58 SUCCESSFUL HARVARD ADMISSIONS ESSAYS

American Publishing House

American Publishing House LLC
30 North Gould Street Suite #4000
Sheridan, WY 82801
www.AmericanPublishingHouse.com
americanpublishinghouse@gmail.com

Ordering Information:
Quantity sales. Special discounts are available on quantity purchases by corporations, associations, U.S. trade bookstores, wholesalers and others. For details, contact the publisher at the address above.

Printed in the United States of America
ISBN 978-0-9973534-0-2 (hardcopy)
ISBN 978-0-9973534-1-9 (electronic)

This book is dedicated to you, the college applicant.

May your college experience provide you with

boundless opportunities and enriching experiences to enable a meaningful life.

Table of Contents

Introduction

Prior to receiving an acceptance into Harvard University, every person featured in this book stared at a blank word document and agonized over the task of convincing admission officers that they should be accepted. It's a frustrating task - pouring your heart and soul into an essay, making all of the edits suggested by a guidance counselor and parents, then realizing that the piece has been taken in an entirely different direction. While your friends appear to have nailed down their applications and entire college admissions strategy, you may still be mindlessly clicking through websites of potential colleges, wondering if you will be accepted anywhere, let alone the college of your dreams. We know the feeling - we were there not long ago. As recent Harvard graduates, we reflected on what would have been most helpful to us while going through the college admissions process and trying to understand what makes applications truly stand out. We realized that something was missing from the how-to guides and friendly advice from school counselors and relatives: the ability to read raw, unedited, and recent essays from successful college applicants. So, we went to our peers and fellow Harvard students and aggregated successful admissions essays into a book to help you on your journey.

When most high school students and their parents think of Harvard, they think of a university that seems worlds away from their list of target and safety schools. They think of a university that only admits students who are already on the brink of an amazing science discovery, applicants who are building the next big drone app to take over the world, or seventeen year-olds who are making a splash in the Olympics while taking on four full-time jobs, and doing all of this in a handstand position. We had the same perception when we were applying to college.

While we did meet some of these students during our time at Harvard, what we also found was that many peers did not, in fact, accomplish countless inhuman feats in their high school years. Rather, they were all extraordinary in their own ways: they were passionate about mentoring others in their communities, ambitious in their pursuits to change society and shape the world. Certainly they are incredible individuals and, after reading their essays and speaking with them about their Harvard experiences, what we found was a common denominator of being genuine, passionate, and reflective in their approach to life. These qualities were represented clearly in their essays.

The college admissions process has gotten more competitive,

complicated, convoluted with every passing year. Instead of taking the SAT or ACT just once, students take the tests multiple times and even hire different tutors for each section of the exams; instead of simply writing college essays and having a couple of friends read through them, students construct multiple variations of each essay and ask family, extended family, friends, and acquaintances to review and edit; instead of only applying to schools that students are truly excited about attending, they now strategically plan a balanced portfolio of safety, target, and reach schools. Make no mistake - we are not bemoaning the process and glorifying a state of the past, but we are acknowledging that the landscape has changed. With the seemingly interminable amount of advice students get, from distant uncles, local college consultants found on craigslist, and books on "How to write a successful college essay" in the dark corners of a bookstore, the process only gets tougher as students try to craft the perfect essay that satisfies the opinions of everyone around them.

When we were considering this project, we asked ourselves "If we had to redo the entire process over, what would we give to our past selves to make it easier?" One of the biggest struggles we encountered during our application process was a dearth of successful admissions essays to show us what works and what doesn't. With all the abstract comments and advice given by guidance counselors and teachers, what we need is a raw and unedited collection of concrete examples. We found our answer in this book - a modern, effective, and illuminative guide to crafting your own Harvard tier essay. Aside from the enlightening aspects of the essays, one of the things we love most about this book is how recent and relevant it is to high school students - these are not essays written in years past, but rather winning pieces that gained an applicant a letter of admission to Harvard University not long ago. Follow what works.

Having helped hundreds of high school students and their families with their college admissions needs, we are often asked this deceivingly simple question: "How do I get into X school?" And we feel obligated to let them know that, because there so many moving parts involved in the application process and there is so little time to address all of the components, there is no one size fit all action that they can do. While EmpiricEdge, the college admissions consulting business we are associated with, addresses the bulk of these issues - building up the resume, displaying leadership experiences, selecting a fitting set of colleges, obtaining glowing recommendations, participating in meaningful extracurricular activities at school and in the community - without the right portrayal in the essays, the student's accomplishments and achievements can lose their effectiveness. As the rest of this book will hopefully show, finding your own voice and reflecting upon your own values and unique attributes are crucial to mastering the essay portion of every application. It's easy to get bombarded with advice, edits, and opinions of those around you - but remember that no one can better understand who you are than yourself. Find your voice in your essays, and don't lose it. This genuine voice will be the guiding light to your success in the application process.

To apply, attend, and graduate from Harvard - or any higher education institution - is a gift. A good education is one of the best gift that one can be given, and one of the few things that can never be taken away. Our alma mater has given us so much. We entered Harvard as high schoolers in pursuit of our dreams, and graduated with resources and a community that serve as a strong foundation for the rest of our lives.

Now, we want to give this same opportunity to all of you. We believe that, no matter what gender, race, country of origin, or beliefs you may hold, you deserve and should have a chance to receive a quality education. We, students from different economic, racial, and national origins, have shared our heartfelt stories and poured them into our application essays, and we now want to give them to you with an open heart. We hope that you feel inspired to take action, and we are ready and excited to guide you through the adventure of getting into a great university.

From our hearts to yours,
Jordan Tung & Kevin Jain

1. "Scars" by Mercedes Flowers

My life wouldn't be the same without my scars. They are my teachers and reminders, bold highlighters of my past and what I've learned from it. Evaluating even a fraction of them provides a cross-section of my history; they signify mistakes, lessons, tribulations and trials- but no matter the story behind them, their meaning is always more than just skin deep.

The first permanent mark on my body came in a three-pack. When I was five years old, my family sought a drastic answer to knee problems that had been ailing me since birth. This came through rare surgery in Atlanta, leaving three thick scars on my left leg.

Spending kindergarten in a wheelchair and summer in crutches taught me the value of mental resilience. At an age when all should be rosy, I faced the reality that life doesn't always go according to plan. More importantly, I learned that although I couldn't always anticipate life's events, I certainly could control my reaction to them; the vast importance of a good attitude became apparent. Looking back at pictures of that time, I'm proud to smile back at the gap-toothed grin that meets me.

The operation, though, was botched. It left my knee with too little cartilage, resulting in arthritis. An internal scar, this kept me well-acquainted with ibuprofen and prevented me from playing sports. But while my friends gallivanted, I found other things to do. I read, reflected, talked, fostered musical interests- I refused to let the scar keep me down.

My freshest scars are forming even now, as I type this essay.

In a September accident, I fell from seventeen feet, breaking both ankles. Spending two days in the hospital, learning I wouldn't walk unaided for three months, and celebrating my eighteenth birthday in a wheelchair was certainly not my vision for senior year. But that's alright. I'm not angry or caustic. I'm thankful. The situation has taught me much about the independence and strength living inside of me.

Life isn't always about ease. I've learned that life is about taking the circumstances given and making astute choices in that light. Knowing that serious injury, even death, could have occurred if my fall's trajectory was only slightly different is incredibly sobering. Even with impairments, I value every day as gift, as an opportunity to make some positive impact on the world. Learning to make the best of a situation, big or small, is paramount in my worldview.

These are only my first and most recent scars, respectively. Certainly, these aren't the last I'll accrue, for I haven't faced life's every pitfall or learned all of its lessons. Superficially, scars are simply fibrous tissue, but to me, they're more than that. They're a vital part of my story, constant reminders of where I've been, where I am, and where I'm going. Yes, my history holds difficulties, but it does not harbor a single regret or bitter vestige; my scars help bring this to mind every day.

2. "Nothing" by Madison Deming

Nothing.

Staring into the eyes of my scene partner, I frantically beat against the black curtain that had suddenly closed over my brain.

"But the possibility for a cure was left open!" my partner repeats, wide-eyed and panicked.

Nothing.

The seconds seem like hours. This mistake is crucial. This mistake is devastating.

Once again: "The possibility for a cure was left open …."

Nothing.

Nothing can ruin everything.

Here, at the national competition of National History Day, my group is up against historical performances from 49 other states and several countries. And my failure can put an end to eight months of nonstop research and rehearsal. My failure can make it all worthless. Nothing.

I have been acting since I was six. Never before have I completely forgotten a line during a performance. I have four partners who have put their hearts and souls into this project depending on me, four people who worked tirelessly with me for the entire school year to get primary interviews, gather sources, and rehearse the performance over and over – and this is when I decide to draw a blank.

Finally my line comes to me. Not from behind that damn black curtain, but from behind our carefully constructed set. From my best friend.

"A consequence of that belief!" she shouts, knowing, as only she can, exactly what I need to continue the performance.

"A consequence of that belief is that people continued to search for a cure to a disease that didn't exist …."

The curtain in my mind lifts and I am back, reciting the lines exactly as we had rehearsed. After the final bow and our interview with the judges, there is nothing left to do but ask myself what went wrong.

The question tortured me for months. The answer? Nothing. I made a mistake, one that I could not have predicted or avoided. It may have seemed disastrous at the time, but it helped me realize something that many people are forced to learn in places far from the sheltered suburbia I call home.

Nothing can ruin everything.

No mistake or hardship can stop the world from turning, and dwelling on my mistakes will do no good unless I take the time to learn from them. There are calamities far worse than forgetting a line in a competition. I did not commit a felony, kill an innocent person, or lose a loved one. We may not have moved on to the final round of competition, but we did become experts on a topic that we were extremely passionate about, and we were able to show that commitment to our judges and peers despite the few seconds of silence.

I went on to compete in National History Day for the rest of high school, getting to the national level three times and placing at the state level four times. Each year brought with it lessons in research, time management, and perseverance. Yet none of it affected me quite as much as those few seconds of silence that June of ninth grade.

Since then I have failed my first test, gotten my first B+ on a report card, had three actors drop out of the show I was directing the day before the performance, and gone through numerous break-ups, breakdowns, and fall-outs. Those few seconds followed me, reminding me every day that I am not the sum of my mistakes, but rather the sum of the lessons I gain from them. Those few seconds of silence should not and will not define my National History Day experience, just as a missed homework assignment, a bad test grade, or a forgotten line will not define me.

3. "The Meaning of Ishkabibble" by Jake Stepansky

You can order a brownie sundae just about anywhere. It's a pretty easy dessert for a restaurant to serve – all you need are brownies, ice cream, and generous helpings of hot fudge – so, no matter where you go, it's just not that hard to find this particular indulgence on the menu.

The Highland Lodge in Greensboro, Vermont is seated at the edge of the woods way up north near the Canadian border. The main building is poised at the side of a winding road, inviting weary travelers inside for a comfortable, homey stay. Farther up on a hill, the rustic, worn cabins are surrounded by tall grasses and flowers, and colorful paintings on wooden plaques, made by children who have long since grown up, hang on the trees.

My family has had the privilege of spending one week in this idyllic corner of the world every summer for the past nine years. We have met and become the closest of friends with two families, returning each year to vacation with them once more. We spend our days relaxing at the beach, walking through the picturesque Vermont countryside, and, of course, eating. And every night, we eat a dessert of almost unspeakable beauty: The Ishkabibble.

What is an Ishkabibble, you ask? Well, actually it's just a brownie sundae. But not just any brownie sundae! It's a brownie sundae fashioned with love and tradition and warmth and heart. An Ishkabibble is so much more than just vanilla ice cream resting atop a warm square of chocolate cake and smothered in rivers of fudge. It's a brownie sundae that represents the bonds of loyalty and affection among the Lodge's returning families, one that embodies a passionate and dedicated determination to preserve old-time values and a pace of life that forgoes busy-ness in favor of finding time for the beauty of human relationships.

Ishkabibble. In Yiddish, "ish kabibble" is a slang term that means "no worries" – something like a Hebraic-Germanic version of "Hakuna Matata." The phrase perfectly characterizes the weeks we have spent in Vermont. Every morning, whenever I would head down to breakfast on the front porch, it would always strike me how lucky I was to be exactly where I was, in such an unspoiled place, surrounded by loving friends and family. There was never any pressure to be someone I was not, never any storm clouds hanging over my head or tensions about the future. I could just *be*.

One night at dinner, I was in the mood for something extra sugary. And so, half-jokingly, I asked for an Ishkabibble topped with everything they had in the kitchen. The waitress, a glint in her eye, smiled and went off to make my dessert. A few minutes later, she emerged bearing an Ishkabibble topped with whipped cream, chocolate shavings, butterscotch sauce and – to my horror and amusement – a black olive, a cherry tomato, and a slice of raw onion. From that time onward, one night each year during our annual stay, my friends at the Lodge would take it upon themselves to order my dessert for me. And every year, I would find it laden with pickles, peppers, and other *delectable* toppings. Although I dreaded that night each time around, I also loved it – and would gladly suffer through an Ishkabibble smothered in Tabasco sauce if it meant I could have the pleasure of being with these same friends in this perfect place even one day each year.

Ishkabibble. Sam Lewis and George Meyer wrote a popular song in 1913 titled, "Isch Gabibble (I Should Worry!)," which later inspired comedian Merwyn Bogue to name his radio alter ego "Ish Kabibble." Throughout the 1930s and 40s, "Ish" lit up the airwaves with his comical shtick as a regular on bandleader Kay Kayser's variety show, the kind of radio broadcast that one could easily imagine wafting out of an old wireless perched atop a shelf in the quaint living room of Highland Lodge for its guests' leisurely enjoyment. Nowadays, the Lodge boasts only one spotty, outmoded, and oft-ignored television set occupying an antiqued sidetable in its front parlor room, but in 2008 - the year our annual trip took place during the Beijing Summer Olympics - it was the main attraction as we crowded around it nightly to watch Michael Phelps break world records. When the champion swimmer finished off the final victorious race of his prodigious season, we all rose up and gave each other great bear hugs, as if *we* had all just won gold medals. For it was enough of a prize to be able to spend time with each other, marking important moments indelibly in our hearts and minds by experiencing them together.

Ishkabibble. When it comes to pleasurable eating, there's really nothing much better than a hot brownie - the way it melts in your mouth, the way it warms your whole body, the way it goes down easy like a spoonful of sugar. And in the same way, nothing has been more deliciously filling – and fulfilling – to every member of our family than this one week in the Vermont woods. For this is a week without cell phones, without Internet access, or even snail mail, and, consequently, without the constant emails, texts, tweets, Facebook posts, phone calls, bills, appointments, meetings, or notifications that blanket our lives on a daily basis. It has been a way to be transported back to a time when there wasn't always something to do or somewhere to be. And when such things do not bind us, we are able to be better human beings. We are able to find joy in the small things in life: the connections we make, the people we meet, the adventures we have – and the brownie sundaes we eat together.

Three months ago, Highland Lodge announced that it was closing its doors. Years of financial struggle for the proprietors' family had challenged their tenacity and dedication to keeping the Lodge running, as their old-fashioned, folksy style of innkeeping had become less and less sustainable; now, they knew the time had come to close their creaky yet sturdy doors once and for all. And just like that, an era of lazy summer afternoons, of home-away-from-home-cooked meals, and of the purest tranquility our family had known, came to an end. There were no blaring news headlines or final trumpet fanfares. The Highland Lodge just, simply and quietly, was gone.

I have come to realize that all those years of eating Ishkabibbles at the Lodge taught me well about what makes life truly sweet. The Ishkabibble recipe is really very simple. We can re-create it in our own homes, and whenever or wherever we find true friends, its ingredients cannot be hard to find. Although the scenery around that cozy, intimate inn in Vermont was postcard-perfect, the true beauty of the place lay much deeper than its captivating exterior. For at the Highland Lodge, we were a family of families and friends. At the Highland Lodge, we could take time to hear our own thoughts and to savor each other's. And I have "ishkabibble" about the way in which the traditions, timeless friendships, and loving community that blossomed there will continue to guide the lives of those who were able to experience the magic of this special place together.

4. "The Scarlet Letter Book Review" by Javier Gutierrez

Out of all the high school books I have read, I believe I felt the greatest degree of attitude change after reading Nathaniel Hawthorne's The Scarlet Letter. In short, Hawthorne's novel is about a woman named Hester Prynne who must live in contempt of society for having committed adultery; her shame persists through a scarlet letter "A" she wears on her dress and her illegitimate daughter, Pearl. This novel, although set in the mid-1860s, reveals many mechanisms of society today. I learned much about how social norms work and the concept of expression in society. In short, if one does something "different" than what is expected, that person is looked down upon.

For example, if a man decides to wear a pink shirt and yellow jeans in public, I am sure there will be people who will prejudge the man and look down on him, regardless of how "unfair" the judgment may be. One may say "But Javier, that man has the right to wear whatever he wants. He has free will and he should not care about what others think!" If all of society thought like this, the world would be a much better place. But such a romanticized ideal is not likely to become the status quo anytime soon. In Hester's case, her Puritan community shames her publicly and declares her adultery as proof of her predestination to go to Hell. Although such scorn is rare today, public disapproval is still a force to reckon with.

Many people believe the right to free expression is a gift - and I agree - but only if used correctly. After reading this novel, I learned that truly free speech may in fact be an illusion. One must usually conform to social norms to some degree lest they are stigmatized, or worse, ostracized by society. As a social being, humans cannot afford to be alienated from society. Therefore, if one wishes to express their opinion or perform a certain action, one should always keep their audience in mind. I believe that only with compelling evidence, significant public support, or respect does one have a fighting chance at altering the status quo or social norms. These three prerequisites reflect the three main forms of rhetoric: logos, pathos, and ethos, respectively.

This idea of free expression has connections with many different aspects of human life. From censorship to revolutions, the right to express oneself is the key force behind such phenomena. Many people feel it's their right to speak freely, but at times that right can infringe on others' happiness or freedom. The biggest question that comes to mind is what will be the ultimate fate of society. In Ray Bradbury's Fahrenheit 451 and Lois Lowry's The Giver, society is depicted as a methodical, censored world devoid of emotion and creativity. Although democracies worldwide are trying to implement free speech platforms, intolerance for foreign beliefs and sensitive topics continue to burgeon. The question is: when will we pass the point of no return?

5. "My Back-Yard Cabin" by Jeffrey Durand

A few summers ago I built a cabin in the secret, inaccessible corner of our yard. This was my first life-size project, larger than all the birdfeeders, models or contraptions I loved making. I wanted it to be the clubhouse for my new nature club, a space where my dreams of playing and working with my friends would come true. Yet things did not turn out the way I hoped they would.

My parents were building a house that summer, and building palettes of all shapes and sizes were starting to litter the yard. I decided to recycle this free material, measured the palettes, and finally worked out a detailed plan for the cabin. The moment of conception was greatly exciting; I could truly let my imagination free.

Then I rallied my two best buddies, Elliot and Douglas, and started building this grand cabin. Virtually every building material was recycled. The stray nails were hammered back into shape and reused. The edges sawed off the ends of the palettes were employed to attach wall parts together. I only used hand tools, refusing power tools that I knew how to manipulate. I simply had decided this was the most proper and fun way of working, and once set on a principle I usually stick to it, even if in this particular case it meant more work.

Almost every day during the whole summer I worked with thrill in the garden. Soon enough the cabin was finished. I was very proud of it, having needed almost no help from my parents and only one pack of nails.

But the project never went past that point. Soon after my best friend, Douglas, moved away to Scotland. Elliot, a year older than me, was soon busy with other things. The club simply never happened. For a long time, I have blamed myself for the failure, feeling I did not do enough for the club's realization. All the while the cabin sat untouched in the yard but I refused to take it down.

Several years passed, and soon the roof of the cabin was too low for me, as if I had started going beyond. I realized that it had not been such a failure after all. While the abandoned club was a fact of life, a question of time and place, the successful building of the cabin had been among the great moments of my youth.

I have not stopped using my imagination. I found a new friend with a passion for building as great as mine. We have worked on all sorts of projects including water rockets that we launched and a collapsible boat with which we went down a river. I have moved forward; this summer I accepted to take the cabin down.

University is the place where I want to meet more people who love creating and working on projects. I want to have the means, this time, to achieve my dreams.

6. "History" by Anonymous

Choosing a history concentration was the easiest college decision I've made so far. I want to know more about how other people around the world live, and what reasons exist in the past for the culture of the present. Part of this fascination feels almost innate. As a young child, my "dream jobs" included photojournalism and archaeology, indicating an early interest in understanding other people. Another part of my attraction to history comes from some adult influences in my life: two art historians for parents (those long hours in museums and confusing dinner table conversations were quite a lot to handle when I was younger, but I appreciate them now), two truly inspiring history teachers in high school, and a grandfather who is both my dearest role model and a well-known global historian. Papa, my grandfather, was a child in Tokyo during World War II and then came to the United States as an undergraduate, eventually becoming president of the American Historical Association. His life taught him that gaining a nuanced understanding of cultures outside of one's own is essential to becoming a well-rounded and thoughtful person, and he took care to pass that lesson on to me. I aspire to see the world's complexities as fairly and insightfully as he does. It is evident to me that to work toward this goal, I should begin by following in his footsteps at Harvard.

A third factor that has drawn me to history has been my experience travelling around the world. One of the greatest gifts my parents have given my sister and me is the chance to explore the globe, offering me an idea of the planet's vastness and a taste of the cultural and ideological diversity it holds. As I become familiar with new places, I also see how much more there is out there to investigate. The best example of this was the semester my family spent living in Paris in 2008. Though I was only twelve, and not really old enough to appreciate just how incredible this opportunity was, it was still the best semester of my life. There was something truly wonderful about developing a day-to-day routine in a place that felt, initially, so different from my hometown. The language, the school system, the Metro, buying fresh baguettes twice a day, the city's bustling activity and rich traces of history became normal after a few weeks. That experience demonstrated to me not only how much fun it was to dive into a foreign culture, but also how quickly I could learn to fit in. However, even as these realizations came to me, new possibilities opened up. I might have mastered everyday life in Paris, but I saw that I was only scraping the surface of the city's rich culture and heritage. I also grasped that, though Paris had seemed huge and intimidating when I first imagined living there, it was only one small part of the Rest Of The World. Undoubtedly Paris is exceptionally wealthy in history and opportunity, but even so, it was just one dot out of thousands on a map. The more I realized this, the less I was able to imagine the massive scope of things I might one day also have the opportunity to learn about and experience.

That semester in Paris greatly impacted who I am today, opening me up to new possibilities and new ideas about the world and my place in it. My hope is that I can have a similarly enriching and exhilarating experience in college, broadening my perspective and deepening my understanding of the world. Where I stand now, well into my senior year in high school and preparing to leave my family and friends behind for the first time, is one of the most exciting places I've ever been. I am ready to explore independently, and I want my path to start in a new city, away from home, where I will be challenged by creative, intelligent people with all kinds of different backgrounds and experiences. I feel like everything I've done so far has been preparation for this opportunity to follow my passions freely and grow in new ways. I hope to do this at Harvard.

7. "Failure" by Anonymous

At 9:15 PM on September 7, 2013, I was parked alone in my car when the cast list for my final performance of "The Nutcracker" with the <Name of Ballet redacted per author's request> was posted online. As I scrolled nervously through the PDF, my anxiety came to a head. It took me about five minutes to read the whole thing. When I finally finished it, I didn't know what to think. I had gotten good parts, but for the third year in a row, I hadn't received the lead role of the Sugarplum Fairy, and it made me feel completely lost.

I joined the Ballet when I was in fourth grade, late for a dancer, because I had seen my best friend perform as a mouse in "The Nutcracker" and wanted to go onstage in front of a cheering mass of people too. Since then, ballet had become one of the most defining parts of my character. I felt that the literally thousands of hours I had spent at the ballet studio were directly linked to specific qualities I valued in myself, such as drive, dedication, and maturity. My passion for ballet was such a part of me that I didn't question why I devoted so many hours to it or what it really gave back to me. But in the days following the "Nutcracker" casting, as I accustomed myself to the fact that years of effort had not be enough to win me the top spot, I reflected on those very things.

At first, part of me wondered if the enormous investment I had made in ballet was worthwhile, but I quickly saw that my commitment to ballet had not wavered. I still worked harder at ballet than at anything else in my life. This reminded me that ballet was about much more than anything an audience might see. The things I cherished most about it—the extraordinary flow that develops during an intense class, the strong sense of community, the rush of appearing on stage—all remained the same. I loved ballet for itself, not for any special recognition that might come with it.

But more than anything else, I realized that for me, the greatest fulfillment in ballet came from teaching. For over a year, a class of seven- to nine-year-olds had known me as "[name redacted]," and my connection to them was one of the most enriching aspects of my ballet experience. I was passionate about teaching because it allowed me to share my love for ballet and the knowledge I had gained from my years of study with dancers who might, one day, grow into such roles as the Sugarplum Fairy. The reward of seeing my students' progress and the fun they had in class was something I would not find anywhere else. All the work I put in felt worth it many times over when I saw my students pushing through the same things I once struggled with. Maybe they could even take the lessons about dedication and hard work that I hoped to share and apply them to their lives in a broader sense. I knew with certainty that teaching was something I was good at, the place where my talent really lay. My teaching position was something no other company dancer had ever been entrusted with. It was where I felt valued most in the company. Teaching was, in the end, the part of ballet I cared most about and the part that had given me the most back. I still felt the sting of being cast second best, but I saw that I already lived my "Nutcracker" dream, and I had the incredible opportunity to pass the experience on to other people.

8. "Another Step Forward" by Hirsh Jain

I was working for four hours and then I realized there was a counter-example and now, well, now it isn't even true. Maybe...maybe math isn't for me. I feel like such a waste, four hours of nothing and I've gotten nowhere and now what..."

I don't often get to play the big brother role at math camp. This was an exception. I gave Rachel a hug, wiped the tears off her face, pulled a notebook out of my backpack, and began to recount my own experience from the previous summer.

After opening it to a page decorated with exclamation points and a huge box around the final line of a proof, I smiled and described to Rachel the elation of showing trivial algebraic closure and definable closure to be equivalent. Four weeks, eight sub-theorems, and countless hours later, my partner, Raj, and I had finally come to the desired result. Moreover, this proof was a stepping stone to any hope of expanding our results to previously undiscovered work.

The following day, Raj and I received an e-mail from our research mentor, which read: "It seems that I've made a mistake. The definition of algebraic closure in the project description reads incorrectly. See the updated attachment." 22 words, and four weeks had just slipped down the drain. Everything we had done was completely invalidated by three sentences. Tearful frustration, pillow punching, and angry games of Angry Birds in the solitude of my room filled the next three days. How could he just give us the wrong definition? How could the work we had done be useless? I smirked at the notebook which had once exhilarated me, crumpled the pages, and tossed it – along with the entire project – aside.

The notebook resurfaced a few weeks later, taunting me from the bottom of a just-emptied suitcase. I snatched it and flipped through the pages, again lamenting about the wasted effort, the wasted time, the wasted thought. After a few minutes, I found myself immersed in the waste; I straightened out the pages, pieced together lemmas and eliminated what was debunked by the misstated definition. Suddenly, this structure elicited the emergence of new exclamation points – the old approach needed only to be slightly altered! I called Raj to show him my discoveries. The phone call fostered new ideas, which enabled us to prove not only the stepping stone theorem, but to achieve new results. In a matter of weeks, these ideas and proofs had turned into a research paper.

The moment when everything came together was beautiful – our efforts, after all, had not been futile. Yet, as I emphasized to

Rachel, I was an abandoned notebook away from missing that completely. As I flipped the notebook shut, I pointed out the taped sheet of paper on the back panel with a quote by Thomas Edison, who I've always admired for his vigorous approach to creation: *I am not discouraged, because every wrong attempt discarded is another step forward.*

9. "School Playground" by Anonymous

My friend bought a jetliner and flew it alone to Seattle to visit the Boeing factory that weekend. And that wasn't the first time. "That's awesome dude!" I said as Daniel modestly shifted his head down, trying to hide the smile that told me he knew he was the coolest kid in school. He sat down on the grass to open his yellow Tupperware and grabbed a slice of pizza, no crust. It's always either pizza or corndogs or pesto pasta, and it's always at our same spot.

"What'd you do this weekend, [redacted]?" he asked, confidently pushing through his speech impediment.

"Oh you know, just studied for my tests and stuff," I told him, consciously concealing all of my experiences he so badly wished he could have as a mentally challenged teenager, like my baseball game and my friend's birthday dinner. He ran out of things to ask me and we started eating. A group of my baseball teammates dropped by to give me some bro hugs while I, for that moment, pretended Daniel was invisible. When all of them were gone, I turned around to my Circle of Friends buddy who was sitting there, eating and waiting.

"I can pitch 100 miles per hour now, [redacted]," he eagerly boasted.

"Nice bro, I'm only throwing about 80." The corners of Daniel's lips crept slightly upwards. He bit into his pizza. I ate my sandwich. Together we looked up at a lone plane buzzing high above us. Suddenly, from somewhere in the depths of his brain, Daniel got an idea.

"Let's play hot hands!" he shouted as he shot up. I caught a glance of a group of seniors pacing by us, watching us, keeping their distance as though an invisible force field stopped them from coming too close. *Really? Hot hands? Here? Now?* Daniel just stood there, palms up and ready, gazing right into me with that awkward expression on his face that never really faded. I hesitantly got off the ledge and rested my palms right on top of his, engulfing his hands in mine. Immediately after I set them down, he struck the back of my hands. In his eyes, I could see his pure triumph from catching me off guard.

"There's no way you're gonna get me this time!" I exclaimed as we reset. I slowly placed my hands back on top of his. Kids walked by us. I could feel their stares. I could sense their muffled laughter. But Daniel didn't care what they thought— he never did. I realized I had to finally let go, to be free like Daniel. I allowed him to smack my hands again and again and again, and laughed with him every time at his victory. I could have done that all day long.

The lunch bell sounded.

I was starting to walk to class with a couple of friends and quickly turned to remind him about next week. "Hey, so I'll see you next Tuesday, alright man?"

"Okay [redacted], I know," he reassured me like he always does. Before I had walked any farther, he told me I could fly with him in his jetliner to the Boeing factory next weekend.

Right there, in the midst of the flood of students, I shouted, "That would be so awesome dude!" and ran back to give him a big bro hug.

10. "My Sister Sierra" by Vegas Longlois

Although my sister, Sierra, and I were practically raised as twins, many of my classmates have trouble believing we are even related. In their defense, Sierra and I are incredibly different. While Sierra is tall, Hispanic and athletic, I am short, Caucasian and physically the weakest person on the debate team. While Sierra is adept at social situations, I am more at home in a library. In spite, or perhaps because of, these differences, my sister is one of the most influential people in my life.

When my family first adopted Sierra (she and I were both three), she was suffering violent withdrawals from medically unnecessary psychiatric medication. In addition, Sierra only spoke Spanish, and a limited amount at that and did not know her colors, numbers, or even how to spell her own name. As such, by the time I began learning how to read, I was helping teach my sister English. In elementary school, I often stayed at the kitchen table after I finished my homework to help Sierra with hers, because her severe dyslexia made school very difficult. When I began to truly conceptualize my career plans, I realized I wanted to be a pediatric psychiatrist in order to prevent another child from suffering like my sister had. To this day, I tutor fellow students because I want someone to do the same for Sierra if she ever needs help. Just last week, a student I had never met before sat down next to me at lunch and asked for help with her Chemistry homework because she apparently knew of my reputation, that I tutor Chemistry almost every morning and will help anyone who asks. Although it meant I did not finish my lunch, I helped her. Because of my sister's obstacles, I realized what I want most in life is to help people.

Frequently, many of my classmates ask me why Sierra isn't in AP classes or a member of an honor society. For years I struggled to find the right answer. Although my sister only once made a hundred on a math test, she is one of the smartest people I know. She can navigate any social situation and has an infallible sense of direction. Sierra forces me to reevaluate what intelligence means, finally giving me the answer to my classmates' questions. Intelligence isn't confined to the ability to win a spelling bee or do well on the SAT. Intelligence includes a multitude of skills and abilities and one would be hard pressed to find a person who didn't possess at least one of these; my sister possesses many. The proudest moment of my life isn't qualifying for the national debate tournament or being told by my principal that I am a National Merit Semifinalist; it is hearing Sierra sing with our school's elite choral group and being able to say,

"That's my sister!"

Finally, being raised as the twin of someone who didn't even speak my language taught me what acceptance truly is. Acceptance isn't tolerating or even admiring people different than oneself, it is knowing these differences don't matter in the grand scheme of life. Not only is my sister adopted, but also nine of my grandmother's thirteen grandchildren are adopted and of a different ethnicity. As such, when I entered kindergarten, I didn't know what race was, let alone that some considered it an important difference among people. I was raised to believe people were simply people. This whole-hearted acceptance of people's differences is one of the things that unites my family. When a gay-straight alliance was formed at our high school, Sierra and I were two of the first people to join, despite the worried questions and disparaging remarks that came our way. We feel compelled to stop discrimination and promote acceptance.

Though many of my classmates initially have trouble accepting that Sierra and I are siblings, once they do they can't believe they ever thought otherwise. Everyone can see the indelible mark her influence has left on me and mine on her. We are inseparable.

11. "Food" by Vegas Longlois

Last Thanksgiving, if asked what I was most thankful for, I would have said food, to be specific, gluten-free food. While food is an essential part of Thanksgiving for almost every American, it really matters to me. Food represents family and my grandmother's attempts at making gluten-free cookies, inventiveness and my mom's cornbread made with applesauce, but most of all, food represents tolerance.

Ironically, food companies weren't always tolerant of food allergies. Until 2009, gluten was disguised on nutrition labels as "modified food starch" or "maltodextrin." A fast-food corporation mislabeled their French fries as gluten-free and unintentionally made thousands of gluten-intolerant Americans ill (myself included). Very few restaurants had allergy-friendly menus.

As I grew older, I began to see society's response to my food allergies as a metaphor for the response to all disabilities, especially my mother's significant hearing impairment. I didn't like what I saw. Often when I went to a doctor's appointment with my mother, I felt angry and ashamed of humanity when the doctor made no effort to face her so she could read his lips. And things used to be even worse. Twenty-seven years ago, my mother felt guilty going off to college because she felt as if she was her deaf mother's only means of communicating with the outside world.

Now, as I apply to college, I know my mother has so many more resources than my grandmother did. Recently Netflix added closed captioning to their online movies and within a year Sony will be releasing a device that allows moviegoers with hearing impairments to see the dialogue on the screen. While life with a hearing impairment is still very difficult, it is slowly but surely improving.

The social shift displayed in the world of hearing impairments is magnified tenfold in the world of food allergens. For example, in the past two years, a plethora of gluten-free foods has hit the market and finding food at the grocery store no longer requires a PhD in nutritional science. More importantly, society's perception of food allergies has dramatically changed as well. Previously, I received disapproving glares at church whenever I could not eat communion and I was the only member of my team who had to pack her own food on debate tournaments. I constantly declined food and offended the person offering it because no one remembered what I was allergic to, just that I was allergic to something. Now my church has gluten-free communion wafers and is aware of the dangers of cross-contamination. Now my debate coach specifically stops at the Whole-foods Market if the tournament isn't near any restaurants with gluten-free food. Now friends stop me in the halls to tell me about the latest gluten-free food they found.

And that is why last Thanksgiving I was thankful for food: not only because I was able to make a pecan pie that actually resembled and tasted like pie but also because of the social change, and the changes yet to come, the pie represents.

12. "My Dream" by Lucia Beatriz de Bernando

Another incipient reader in a typical Spanish-speaking home might have relegated *Somos Médicos* to the bottom of the book basket, but not I. The sixteen chunky (and washable) pages chronicled the precocious seven-year-old Ana and her baby brother Luis assisting the doctor as she made her rounds at a hospital where everyone spoke Spanish and most of the patients looked something like me. At the age of four, I decided that I would one day help *Doctora* take the brown-skinned baby's temperature, bandage the little light-haired boy's arm, and hold the older lady's x-ray films up to the bright light. That's not to say that I did not try to keep my options open. When I later acquired the intrepid siblings' further adventures, *Somos Pilotos* and *Somos Zoológicos*, I was briefly led astray by the cunning Ana and Luis, who convinced me to forsake the hospital in favor of a new career as both pilot and zookeeper. However, I soon abandoned all other lines of work and reclaimed my medical calling.

I was born into a family that drinks tea out of hollowed-out gourds through metal straws and eats "special" parts of cows that my American friends didn't know were edible. They sing lively Paraguayan folk songs, the majority of which seems to pay homage to cattle, monuments, Paraguayan dirt, and various types of trees. (As a kid, I seldom invited my classmates to my house after school.)

Paraguay is the second poorest country in the hemisphere, after Haiti. The interior of the country has scant natural resources, limited modern conveniences, and almost nothing to recommend it to the average tourist. The smothering heat, visible in undulating waves, can literally take your breath away. I love the place.

We have made several long and costly trips to Paraguay in recent years, due to a series of unexpected serious illnesses and family tragedies that required us to live there for months at a time. Though these have been occasions of adversity for my mother and her family, I have come to view them, in some measure, as a unique opportunity.

About a year ago, I faced a dilemma. I needed a job, but we had to go to Paraguay again. There is a large Paraguayan company which is comprised of many diverse agricultural and manufacturing businesses. The name is everywhere —on television, billboards and buses. In advance of our trip, I contacted the company (using info located on the label of their *yerba mate* tea), explained my situation, and asked if they had any temporary jobs available. After several weeks of questions and answers, they formally offered me a paid six week internship.

My tasks involved mainly word processing and tabulating sales numbers at first, but I became a volunteer for anything. After that, I was given the more interesting job of translating correspondence for the corporate officers. I worked hard and my resourcefulness caught the attention of my superiors. There were several new product roll-outs while I was there and I was chosen to accompany the vice president to two of the press events as a product model. My name and picture were in three national newspapers.

When the internship was over, I was paid $1,500 instead of the original internship stipend of $500. They told me that I was a "formidable" young woman and that I was welcome to come back to the company. Nothing could have topped my summer experience – except for what happened next. I was surprised when the company's owner remembered our conversation about a free health clinic I wanted to establish. The owner is a very charitable man, and he gave me encouragement and seemed genuinely interested in what I had to say. The company has vast land holdings and commercial interests in all reaches of the country, and when I graduate, his company is going to provide the clinic building. He made me promise never to forget that Paraguay needed me (his words), and said that all I had to bring was my degree.

As someone looking to enter the field of medicine, it bothers me that health and wellness are not issues of concern in the rural areas where my relatives live. In the tradition of the Paraguayan *campesino*, the people are reluctant to seek medical attention, preferring to take the advice of the local *pohãnohára* ("faith healer" in the Guaraní language) for their ailments. My headstrong uncle died last year from an illness that could have been treated, and his father and son (my grandfather and cousin) face the same fate. Because this backward way of thinking has personally affected my family, I am eager to put a stop to this detrimental practice. Medical school has always been on my radar screen, but a few years ago, I was not certain of my path. Now that I have witnessed firsthand what medical knowledge can achieve in third world countries, my dream has a focus.

13. "Mi Familia" by Lucia Beatriz de Bernando

The music coming from the large band section at the front of the room is deafening. As it builds, I can feel the emotions of the expectant crowd pulsating through the air. Last-minute audience members scurry in, naively hoping to grab a seat near the stage but contenting themselves with the plastic folding chairs hastily arranged in the back corners of the already overflowing hall. Just as the band reaches a climactic crescendo, it receives the signal. For five seconds, there is silence. Every head, mine included, turns instinctively to face the back of the room. The music commences anew; the familiar song causes a commotion even greater than the one before. I am singing. Hands clap to the beat and untrained voices around me belt out lyrics unashamedly. Then comes the moment we have all been awaiting: the charismatic protagonist, clad from head to toe in flowing green and gold, starts to process energetically down the center aisle toward the stage, stopping occasionally to shake a fortunate hand. As the music and the crowd reluctantly wind down, he turns to address his devoted audience: *"El Señor esté con todos ustedes."* Collectively, the congregation responds: *"Y con tu espíritu."*

I have been going to Spanish-language Sunday Mass with my family since I was born. In contrast with the formal atmosphere of the English-language services I've attended, the colorful Latino ceremony is a noisy affair. I wonder if the party atmosphere is appropriate, given the solemnity of the occasion. My momentary guilt dissipates as the Merengue beat of the next hymn triggers synchronized hand-clapping, foot-tapping and even some hip-swaying. Conventional church decorum, I conclude, is for English Mass.

There is a middle-aged Anglo couple at this particular service. I suspect they must be new parishioners who didn't realize the 1:00 Mass was not in English. They seem a little fidgety as they survey the boisterous Sign of Peace proceedings: *Abuelitas* in black shawls and dutiful old-timers are bursting out of their pews in every direction to hug or kiss friends (and strangers) on the opposite side of the room, as if long-lost relations from the old country. I seek out the uncomfortable couple and stretch out my hand with a reassuring smile; they reciprocate and look relieved. I am relieved that they are relieved.

Sundays spent at Spanish Mass are my weekly field trip to another land where the warmth, colors and rhythm that make up my story are all around me. I smile as I contemplate the sense of *familia* that envelops the whole church. Those of us with Hispanic backgrounds are bound together by a cultural commonality, and my involvement with our congregation (as a catechism teacher, altar server and lector) has undoubtedly contributed to my perception of what it means to "belong". I feel compelled, in large part by this experience, to exploit the opportunities afforded me in college to not only maximize my success, but to pay it forward to the benefit of my community —*mi familia*.

14. "The Axe Murderer Under the Covers" by Molly Alter

For me, reading is anything but an escape into fantasy. I love gritty and miserable books that include murder, mayhem and family dysfunction. While I have at least some interest in all genres of literature, dark books interest me most. For a long time I couldn't figure out why I like a good shank in the ribs more than a soft caress of the cheek, but I'm developing some theories.

It could be that I like gritty books because of the way I was raised. Nothing like growing up on a nice block in a yuppie town to make me yearn for meaner streets. Soon after listening to my parents read us Maurice Sendak's "Where the Wild Things Are," my siblings and I graduated to the truly scary stuff. My mom's idea of read-aloud books was far from PTA-approved. She read us books like "Compulsion: The Leopold and Loeb Story," Truman Capote's "In Cold Blood," and Jeffrey Toobin's "The Run Of His Life: The People Versus OJ Simpson." Bedtime stories, to the horror of my aunts and uncles, were mostly true crime. Yes, there were the classics like "The Little Prince" and "Rebecca Of Sunnybrook Farm," but they were usually chased down by stories like the one about the "Long Island Lolita,"—Joey Buttafuoco's girlfriend—who shot his wife in the face. My siblings and I were truly sick puppies; we argued about Nathan

Leopold's glasses, Perry Smith's boots, or OJ Simpson's glove. We were tickled to hear about the underside of life as long as it was from under the warm covers of our parents' bed.

As I grew older, I supplemented pulp crime books with those about the underclass. The worlds in Claude Brown's "Manchild in the Promised Land" and Ron Suskind's "A Hope in the Unseen" were as scary as actual crime. As I compared my own upbringing to that of Jeanette Walls, the hungry and neglected character in "The Glass Castle," I felt inexperienced, super suburban, and what might be called "under-deprived." I read that book four times (yes, I'm a repeat offender.) This was not just a story about alcoholic rants and giant rats. Though I would never have wanted to live on the run as the Walls family had, I actually learned something from these charming degenerates. "Home" was not an address; it's family. And family, even parents, could be as cruel as strangers. Reading about this darkness in one childhood illuminated my own.

Many of the adults in my life have dismissed my reading taste as seedy or macabre. But anger, fear, revenge, and duplicity are right there in the Bible and are no less present in contemporary books. Beyond the sordid details, it's the moral quest for justice that appeals to me. For every psychopath, I try to find a dedicated investigator at work. For every neglectful parent, I turn the page to find a caring teacher. For every wrongfully accused man, I look for tales of exoneration. Life in the streets doesn't usually have a satisfying ending, but these books never fail to give me perspective. Next to the gruesome worlds I read about, real life seems downright luxurious. They offer me an unusual form of escape, not into fantasy, but into a reality that many face. The contrast has made me a realistic optimist, a feeling intensified by watching brave characters overcome their circumstances. All the axe murderers and pedophiles of my imagination have had the reverse effect of making me think that there is good in the world. Although I have to say, if a creepy guy in a white van offers me a ride, I'd run like the wind.

15. "A Shake of a Snow Globe" by Molly Alter

When I was little, I collected snow globes. My dad brought them back for me from New York, Chicago, Hollywood, Miami, Tokyo, Rome and elsewhere. They spread out across my dresser top between my tennis trophies and my second-to-last place swimming ribbons; the replicas of great buildings, bridges and Ferris wheels were made even more alluring by being covered in "snow." When I was in elementary school, my friend Diana accidentally broke my biggest globe. I cried as filmy water littered with small flakes seeped into the carpet. In their new exposure, the plastic buildings seemed cheap and inconsequential. Soon, my friend and I moved on to another game.

I myself live in what must strike most people as an artificial globe. My town is safe, I have a great family, and I go to a good school. Sure, there was a tempest in my world when my siblings went to college. Or, in a ferocious shake of the globe, when my dad was diagnosed with non-Hodgkins lymphoma. But in all, I live in a controlled environment where I rarely have to interact with the world beyond my glass sky.

Even in my varied summer experiences abroad, I could still find the solid ground of home. In Queretaro, Mexico, my Mexican "siblings" and I would play basketball just as I do with my brother in New Jersey. In Israel, amid the soldier-lined streets, I could hit the same yellow balls at the same kinds of tennis academies that I know in the United States. Middle class life in foreign countries nowadays resembles home enough to mute the culture shock.

Ironically, it was in New York City, only 12 miles from my dresser top, that I found the most unsettling of my foreign globe experiences. When I stepped out of the 103rd Street and Lexington Avenue subway station on my first day of work, alone in a beaten-down neighborhood where I'd never been, I felt jumpy and disoriented.

I got lost on my way to the East Harlem School (where I was teaching Spanish for the summer) after over-relying on Google Maps. I wandered around the *barrio* timidly asking people for help. Everyone else seemed comfortable, which was no surprise considering that they lived there. But I wasn't. A week later, I saw a man shooting heroin near the JFK Expressway. Another day, some neighborhood kids shouted "Chink" at my Asian-American co-worker and filthy sexual comments at me. I was a long way from being on the outside, looking in. I was in, but on the outside.

Yet over time, I came to appreciate the cast of characters arrayed before me when I walked to work: the man playing Spanish music on a boom box while he sat on a lawn chair on 102nd, the two women who ran the *chucherria* haggling cheerfully in Spanish, and the men at the Pentecostal Church selling children's clothes. Eventually, I worked up the nerve to say hi to them every morning. They greeted me warmly in return.

As I got to know the people in the neighborhood and the kids in my school, I started to relax and open myself up to the vitality of the place. Too bad they don't make snow globes of East Harlem, I thought. But even if they had, I preferred to experience it directly rather than through glass. And those faraway places on my dresser top? Now maybe I can see them through new eyes, too.

16. "Thank you for the Clementines" by Nina Shevzov-Zebrun

With a mug of tea on the table before him, my Russian-speaking, émigré grandfather peels a carton of clementines for my little sister and me. Methodically pulling peels and separating segments, my grandfather always prepares too much fruit. He knows one bowl would suffice—but I suspect he frets that a single bowl on the table might not catch my preoccupied eye as I whiz through the dining room, textbooks in hand, eager to commence my homework.

Until quite recently, I paid little attention to even his most extravagant displays of citrus. Eating the fruit he set out with his granddaughters in mind was simply part of my nightly routine during his visits, as ordinary as practicing Russian or listening to his tales of my émigré ancestors, who came to America as a result of the Russian Revolution with little money and few belongings. But one stuffy night this past spring, I happened to hang by the fruit, nonchalantly thanking my grandfather for the hydrating snack. I saw my grandfather's eyes brighten and laugh. He was pleased I had acknowledged his small act of thoughtfulness. In his thick Russian accent, he offered me some grandparently insight: "I am glad you see what I do for you." Humans do not require much to maintain faith in the worth of their efforts. They simply need reminders that the time they sacrifice from their own lives to benefit others is time appreciated, time well-spent.

I now thank my grandfather for every clementine he peels. Each time he visits, he peels fewer of them before he tires. But that means nothing, for I show I notice his efforts not because I fear a lack of ready-to-eat fruit, but rather because I want to demonstrate that I have absorbed his wisdom, made his words a part of my approach to relationships. Though I only recently received my grandfather's counsel, his teaching has taken root and expanded through my consciousness so now I too find satisfaction in openly recognizing the parts of me that others have instilled, cultivated, molded. I recognize, for instance, and am thankful for my grandfather's role in fostering my sense of Russian identity. He planted in me a desire to remember my family's Russian roots, and I seek to maintain knowledge of the Russian language for him, to keep alive the memory of our relatives who were forced from their homeland and yet, through faith and perseverance, managed to establish themselves in American society. Through opening my eyes to my Russian history, my grandfather gave me the urge to continue my family's heritage of dedication, to work for the welfare of my family. I take comfort knowing he is pleased and proud to be the peeler, the conduit of this Russian "segment" of my character which, as I remind him often, I cherish deeply.

17. "On Point" by Nina Shevzov-Zebrun

The glue-hardened satin fought my toes. My arches lay limp on my pointe shoes' gritty insoles. Try as I might, my eleven-year old feet would not bend those rigid blocks of pink sheen as I endeavored to roll up through the shoes to pointe for the very first time.

Glancing in the mirror at the row of bunheads standing with me along the ballet barre, I saw fellow tongues protruding and lips curling in determination, frustration at the first day of pointe work. Then I saw arches. Beautifully curved, voluptuous arches, molded for ballet from birth. Except for the shoes sagging from my flat feet, all other shoes were already properly molded; the other dancers' high arches—a classical component of ballet aesthetics—had, within seconds, bent each shoe exactly at its center, created the optimal leg line.

I pounded the tip of my ever-rigid shoe on the grey floor they told me was sprung, padded with a bounce to help dancers soar. Piano notes signaled the start of class, but I made sure to remain grounded, flat, secure on my heels for as long as the music would allow. I dreaded the moment I would again see that prescribed perfection around me—those shoes, all agleam and smiling with new satin, mocking me with their curved profiles, reminding me with upturned smirks, "You were not made for this, your feet cannot do this, you are not fit for us."

The studio floor must have heard the shoes' enfeebling insults, for as soon as I came to full pointe, I felt its buoyancy, its resilience rouse and percolate through me. At my sides girls wobbled, ankles teetered, and heels collapsed with the weakness that so often accompanies perfectly-shaped feet. But I remained still, perched and resolute atop my shoes' platforms. The uprightness of my flatter feet firmly supported the weight of my body and heart, let me pose en pointe with elegance despite the worrisome knowledge that the nerve endings in my then-uncalloused toes were ablaze.

My teacher called out to us, the struggling youngsters, to feel the cores of our bodies placed over our second toes. We must be centered, she declared, solid in our positions, not falling askew. But I found I was already standing atop my second toe, my flat yet strong feet having naturally identified my personal balance point. I could support myself even sans barre, for my center was aligned correctly and effectively, positioned rightly. I discovered I did not need the hook-like feet that someone somewhere had deemed desirable, attractive, requisite for ballet; I needed nothing but my properly-placed, wholesome core to hold me en pointe for the entirety of the music.

Since that class eight years ago, I have come to understand that the illusory high arch is an ever-present aspect of human life. Shifting standards of beauty and often impossible ideals, whose origins and aims are frequently forgotten, can captivate and destabilize us. But as I learned that day, an upright core has the power to sustain balance and integrity, to raise us above the pressures of convention on the wings of our individual strengths and abilities. With such an intrinsic sense of center and stasis, I can keep myself aloft interminably, poised above a world so filled with elusive perfection.

18. "Doubly Blessed" by Anonymous

I look upon the scene of a little girl, young and naïve, standing with her brother and sisters in a room that she doesn't know she'll never set foot in again. She also doesn't know that this is the last goodbye she'll ever bid her siblings again. Any bystander would gaze upon these children and take pity on them. However, this bystander wouldn't know what I know. He or she wouldn't know that this is merely God's will being done. I smile because I'm in on a little secret. I *know* what is to become of this little girl. Eleven years later, after having been adopted at the age of six and having left behind all that was familiar to her, this little girl has blossomed into the young lady I am today.

I have come to think of my adoption as the biggest blessing I have ever received from God. I would have never imagined myself as the potential valedictorian of my high school and I would have never imagined all the successes I've had up until this point. I am also of the few lucky ones that have two families. One is simply awaiting our encounter again, the other who has helped me grow into the person I am today, and who has taught me what it truly means to love. I've learned that real love is given freely and from the heart, and not out of obligation or simply because one is kin. My adoptive parents and family love me because they chose to, not because they had to.

I consider my life unique, for I have something to look forward to every day, and it's not just anything, but the one thing that is going to complete my blessed and happy life: my reunion with my biological mother and siblings. "Regular" people don't have this type of motivation; they don't have this one thing to look forward to because they have everything right before them. I, on the other hand, look forward to traveling back to my past and discovering my true identity, especially since my childhood memories are very vague.

There are times, of course, when I wish that I could be with my own, biological family, when I wonder what it's like, when I envy those around me who have this opportunity. But then I remember that if I were like them, I wouldn't be where I am today. My life would probably be completely different, and because this is the life that God intended for me, I wouldn't want it any other way.

As I compare my six-year-old picture with my senior graduation picture, I find it hard to believe that it's the same person. All I know is that everything I have managed to accomplish up until today is attributed firstly to God and secondly to the immense love and support I've received from my family.

19. "Foreign Native" by Anonymous

As I look out the window, a wave of emotions suddenly come over me. The city lights on the hills slowly disappear as the plane flies overhead, and I feel my eyes begin to water. "This is it," I think to myself. "After eight long years, this is it. I'm *finally* home." I begin to feel restless, anticipating the moment I step off the plane and take in my first breath of Colombian air. I am 14 and it is my first time visiting Colombia since I was adopted and moved to the United States at the age of six. I do not remember what it is like living in Colombia, so it will feel like my first time ever there. Will I be a foreigner in my own country?

We arrive at my grandmother's home. It is a small, humble apartment that lacks the luxuries I am accustomed to back at home. I contemplate the idea that a simple life is a happy life, especially if one is with family.

Over the next few days, we do much walking around the city. I love it! As we walk, the sun warms my face, strangers greet us with smiles or hellos, and I get the feeling that I am precisely where I belong. I had been like a lost wolf that had finally found its pack. I was now among *my* people and no longer a minority among Americans. Even with its widespread poverty and ever-present danger, I am convinced that there is not anywhere else that would truly feel like home. For the first time in my life, I experience the extreme sense of nationalism that Americans must feel as they think about their "land of the free"—their colossal love, boundless pride, unifying bonds with one another.

I walk to the small store on the corner to buy a soda one afternoon. The man behind the rails asks me if I am a foreigner. "No," I reply, "I'm Colombian." He states that I have a strange accent that is unrecognizable. "It must be my English accent. Have I really changed that much since I've lived in the U.S.?" I think to myself, disappointed.

I am hurt. I had thought that being back in my home country, I fit in, but this was like a slap in the face—a slap that put me back into reality. The cold truth was that I had been away far too long to stroll in one day and act like I was an ordinary native of Colombia. Perhaps I was overreacting, but I *was* a foreigner and I did not like it.

I love my guerilla-torn country, and I love my colorful culture. The last thing I want is to lose the connection I have with it, for it is a part of me and has influenced who I have grown up to be. I am proud to be different whenever someone asks my ethnicity, and I am proud of the rich stories my mother and grandmother tell about their childhoods—stories that no one else can tell. Doubtless, I *have* changed, but I certainly will not lose my identity as I continue to assimilate into the American culture. I am sure of that.

20. "Untitled" by Jullian Duran

As I sat sweating in a flimsy folding chair waiting for someone to guide me through the school, I wondered who in their right mind actually thought a small ceiling fan would mitigate the engulfing, thick tropical heat. After a few minutes, an administrator approached me and told me to follow him to the first classroom I would be helping. As we walked through the labyrinth of hallways, I noticed several students wandering around and many teachers running late. He led me into the ninth-grade classroom I was assigned to and whispered, "Buena suerte."

It was absolute chaos. Everyone was restless and nobody was in a seat. I greeted the teacher in English, but she did not seem to understand me too well. Switching over to Spanish, I asked her when class would begin. She wondered the same thing. Frustrated at how unorganized everything appeared to be, I walked to the front of the room and began writing out the first paragraph of my last debate case on the chalk board. It seemed to catch the students' attention, and the noise level gradually reduced. When I was done, the room was silent. Feeling like the teacher, I told everyone their assignment for the day was to translate what I had just written on the board.

Noticing their perplexed looks, I explained I would be happy to help if they would just give me their full attention for the next hour.

The students seemed to know a lot more English than I expected. This appeared to be their first challenging assignment. When the bell rang, the teacher stood up and congratulated me. She had many questions about what I had written and asked if I could write down a few more examples in her notebook for future reference. Turns out, after only one class period, it was recess. As we walked toward the teachers' conference room, I asked the teacher why everything was so chaotic. She explained that the Ecuadorian school system was not very rigorous. New laws by the government forced teachers to give fewer tests per month and fewer failing grades. She seemed very angered by it all.

The next two weeks were much like the first day. I walked into a disruptive class, gave the students difficult assignments, and realized the students knew a lot more than expected. Many of them wanted to know more and stayed after class to ask questions. When it came to the teachers, some were passionate about their job, others were indifferent, and most hardly spoke any English. At one point, a teacher called in sick, and I was her only replacement. Regardless of how perplexing the entire arrangement was, I made it a goal of mine to make every class a little more challenging. I suggested the teachers have their students read english books at home, have their students discuss their thoughts about what they read in class, and give their students pop quizzes every so often.

On my last day, the principal called me into her office. To my surprise, every single teacher I helped was there in the office with a cake. We all exchanged contact information, and the principal thanked me dearly for my help. As I walked home, and once again felt the thick tropical heat, I began to think about what I had accomplished in the last two weeks. Even though I still keep in touch with some of those teachers, I wonder how many of them have actually made an effort to make their classes more rigorous. I wonder if I actually convinced a student to try to become fully bilingual. I wonder if anyone at that school will ever realize that a small ceiling fan is a waste if you live near the equator.

21. "Child of an Immigrant" by Jullian Duran

Fretting over small, percentage point deviations in my grades or which evidence should be included in my debate case did not exactly make for good dinner conversation when both of my parents were either studying or working full-time jobs. It is not like I had someone there handing me extracurricular opportunities either. There were always friends and family with me for support, but I was the only one who decided what I would or would not do academically.

As first-generation immigrants, my parents have struggled to get situated in America. The effort has consisted of taking many low-end jobs, living in unpleasant neighborhoods, and getting an education all the while. Money has always been an issue, the cultural barriers never went away, and my parents had to make a completely new network of friends. Keeping all of that in mind, how could I ever ask them to worry about what courses I should take, what grades I should make, or which clubs I should join? I knew from an early age that those were my responsibilities.

Undoubtedly, those responsibilities can become a little daunting if you do not have connections to get you places. Most of the people around me had their parents getting them job offers or internship opportunities. I refused to stand idly by. My starting point was the one place I did not need connections to do well, school. Keeping near-perfect grades meant a lot of careful planning and many late, stressful nights. Getting my long list of accomplishments in debate meant many lost weekends, months of extensive research, and years of fine-tuning my rhetorical skills. When I learned of a job to organize and check-in textbooks at my school over the summer, a friend and I got the school district to hire us. Out of school, my initiative landed me several great opportunities. On an infrequent trip to visit family in Ecuador, I spoke to a principal of a local school and got the chance to be an assistant of the school's English department. After two years of finding ways to make the forty-five minute drive to and from downtown to attend many Mayor's Youth Council events, I got the opportunity to be an intern at City Hall. Since I needed to drive downtown more often, and gas does buy itself, I had to get a job. After talking to the managers of several establishments, I decided to go with McDonald's. There were many other things I did, like volunteer for my local library and become a co-founder of my school's Philosophy Club. None of them, though, were handed to me on a silver platter.

There are probably thousands of highly motivated and dedicated students in the US. I have never met anyone other than myself who is self-motivated and self-dedicated. A college application can list someone's achievements, but I feel like it leaves out what had to happen for those achievements to be realized. Many people can say they were pushed to do well or got an opportunity because of someone else's hard work. In my case, anything academic I have accomplished is because of my work ethic or the connections I have forged. College is a place where most people first experience academic independence. In my case, that has been there, it will stay there, and it can only get better.

22. "Grandma" by Anonymous

The dice weighed heavy in my hand as I scanned the board in front of me. My stomach tightened. I could hardly contain my anticipation. *This is it,* I told myself. Holding my breath, I released the dice in mid-air. They turned over, *once, twice, three times,* and dropped silently, as if suspended in slow motion, finally hitting the board with a series of *clacks*. I stared in disbelief at the combination of black dots, and advanced my dog six spaces. At last, Boardwalk was mine.

From my first encounter with Monopoly at age five, I took more than just a liking to the game. It was beautiful, not merely in its exquisite colors and mathematical complexities, but in its air of unlimited opportunity. Each game was a continuous cycle of investment, guided by my unwavering desire to buy, build, and expand. Through my childhood eyes, the money itself didn't matter. Instead, I saw the board as my canvas, a medium in which I could endlessly create. I never perceived Monopoly as a game of luck, but one of prowess. With each game came a new beginning, and a chance to plunge into unchartered territory.

Mine was an inherited passion passed on to me by my grandmother, who spent countless hours curled up with me on the living room floor making trades, purchasing houses, and laughing contagiously as she recounted stories of her childhood. Born in Brooklyn during the Great Depression and the daughter of Ukrainian immigrants, my grandmother grew up in a world of hardship. Unable to afford college, she spent her young adult life working as a bookkeeper. Forever frugal and an inveterate thrift shopper, she shared her hand-knit sweaters and secondhand "finds" with everyone she knew.

Even in Monopoly, she could not conceal her economic prudence and homegrown concern for others. With each roll of the dice and in each investment, she acted deliberately, favoring middle class strongholds such as Tennessee Avenue over extravagant expenditures, such as Boardwalk and Park Place (my childhood favorites). In games when my money dwindled and I edged toward bankruptcy, she attempted to give me an upper hand, risking her own loss for my gain. However, even as she sought to help me, my high cost hotels would fall victim to her more modest investments. Her subtle approach to the game acted as a guide over the years, causing me to abandon the risky methods my parents once worried would lead me to become a cutthroat Wall Street broker, in favor of a more practical strategy centered upon diversified assets and modest investments.

Six years after her death, my grandmother's philanthropic temperament continues to influence my moral and political beliefs. It took hundreds of hours of engaging in innocent greed to understand my own desire for something more than accumulating vast wealth and power. Instead, I have come to believe that the strength of an individual lies in their regard for others, and that all deserve a piece of Free Parking.

23. "Travel" by Anonymous

Pune to Bangalore. Kanyakumari to Kochi. Mumbai to Delhi. Chennai to Pune. These are just a few of the overnight trains and buses that I have taken during my time in India. The opportunity Mahindra United World College of India grants us to travel—both independently and with the school—is one of its most unique aspects. A huge factor in this mobility is the location of the college. Transport and lodging in India are very cheap if one is willing to sacrifice a few luxuries such as hot showers and air conditioning. In other words, travelling in India is perfect for young students. Though each of my travel experiences has been unique, there is one that particularly stands out—when I travelled overland from Dharamsala to Kathmandu, a 1500km journey, on my own.

At this point, it is necessary to outline my travel plans. I was going to Dharamsala to stay with my friend Konstantin, then to Kathmandu where I would stay with Samarjeet. In both locations, I would meet many MUWCI-ites during their post-grad vacations; in between, however, I would be alone. It was during the journey from Dharamsala to Samarjeet's house that I engaged most with the foreign environment. My plan was to get to Delhi by bus, then take a train to Gorakpur, 90km away from the border with Nepal. Both of those tickets were booked, but after that part of the journey, all I knew was that I would need to find a way to Kathmandu from Gorakpur once I got there. Thus I set off on the ten-hour overnight bus from Dharamsala to the Majnu Ka Tilla Tibetan Settlement in Delhi, where I arrived at 5:00 AM.

After a quick nap in Khan Market and time killing with the help of The Life of Pi, I boarded a crowded train en route to Gorakpur. To my dismay, I found my six-person compartment already inhabited by an entire family of fifteen, ranging from a grandmother to a newborn baby. I put my 65-liter backpack and my gym bag on the top bunk I had booked and climbed on. The next two hours I spent trying to find the best possible arrangement for the three of us. I settled with a gym-bag-pillow and a backpack-footrest. I napped, read, drank chai, and ate Kurkure, a common Indian snack, on my bunk, leaving only for the occasional bathroom trip. At around 9:00 PM, I realized that I had no more credit in my phone, and that I did not know Samarjeet's address. I fell asleep somewhat worried about how I would find him. I woke up at five to make sure I did not miss my stop, which came three hours later. After leaving the train I stood on the platform, looking for any sign of the way to Nepal as a bustling crowd of driven and determined people engulfed me.

"To Nepal only?" The man with henna-died hair rescued me quickly from the sea of passengers, and I made a snap decision to trust him. I followed him through the platform and arrived at a jeep in the parking lot. Inside were four other people, presumably Nepali or North Indian. They welcomed me with smiles as I squeezed in next to them, and half an hour later, we were off. During the two-hour ride, I met a Punjabi man who was also going to Kathmandu. He seemed pleasant. We arrived in Sonauli, on the Indo-Nepali border, about two hours later, and a bicycle rickshaw driver picked me up and guided me through the visa process. The first stop was the Indian exit point, where I was told that my papers were not in order to leave the country. After a brief argument, the man made it clear he required a bribe, which I grudgingly paid. This illegal request by the Indian official was in stark contrast to what happened next at the Nepali visa bureau. I entered the well-lit office, where I found five government officials—a big change from the one crooked man sitting in the dim Indian outpost—paid the correct visa fee, got official stamps, and was on my way to the bus stand. I tried to call Samarjeet from a Nepali phone, but I could not reach him. I boarded the bus still without knowledge of where to go once I arrived in Kathmandu.

Though it was only around 270km away, the ride took more than nine hours. The sweltering heat only aggravated the cramped conditions of the overcrowded bus. Drenched with sweat, I watched in awe as we passed a most fantastic landscape. On my right was a mountain face hundreds of meters high, and on my left was a sheer drop down into a river way below. Like The Little Train that Could, the bus chugged along these roads that seemed too steep for it. I ended up sitting next to the Punjabi man from the jeep, and we made some small talk. I told him that I would be flying home through Bangkok, to which he responded, "Bangkok is good for fun!" I laughed it off but in retrospect it was a clear sign of what was to come. Eventually I realized that I would not be able to get to Samarjeet's that day because I would reach Kathmandu too late. My travel companion told me that he could help me find a guesthouse. I agreed, knowing that his Hindi would help me get a cheaper room. Sure enough, after we got off the bus, a hotel boy approached us, and the Punjabi man managed to cut his starting price in half. Once assured that we would have separate rooms, we followed the boy into a back alley and into a tall building. What happened next is something I'll not soon forget.

As we were being led to our rooms, a girl in short shorts and a tank top passed us, in whom the Punjabi took particular interest. He asked the hotel boy about "girls" in Hindi, and the boy pointed at a door. The Punjabi opened the door, took a look inside, and came back to us visibly impressed. The girls in that room were prostitutes. I was in a brothel. Knowing that it would be hard to find another place to stay at that late hour, I decided to remain at this hotel, which was ironically marked, in Sharpie written on the door, as the "Hilton Guest House." We went inside a room with two beds each supplied with a thin mattress, a pillow, and a blanket. The shower had no light and was in the same room as the Eastern-style toilet. Waiting to receive my key, I stood awkwardly as the Punjabi and the hotel boy bargained about prices for one woman for the night—in my room. The starting price was 3000 Nepali rupees or about 34 US dollars. After what seemed like forever, they left me to myself. I took a quick cold shower, picked the bed that looked least likely to be housing bugs, and slept. I awoke at eight, left as quickly as possible, and found an Internet café. I took down Samarjeet's address and hopped into a cab that took me all the way there. Sixty-four hours after leaving Dharamsala, I finally had reached my destination.

This experience can be summed up by a cliché: "It's not about the destination, it's about the journey." Once at Samarjeet's, everything became much calmer. The only regrets I have relating to the trip have to do with not keeping a cool enough head. At the Indian border office, I paid a much bigger bribe than necessary because I got caught up in the possibility of being stuck in India. I also almost got off the train too early at a stop called "Goraj" because I thought I had heard someone say Gorakpur. My trip was much easier when I just went with the flow of things, and I think in some sense that is the nature of life in India. For example, the extra dorm at our school was supposed to be built before we accepted more students, but due to delays, we now have at least one extra person in about half the rooms. There is nothing we can do except to keep living life and wait. Patience goes a long way in India, especially if you are on a budget. If not, then money talks, as the prevalent corruption demonstrates. Even our school uses some kind of bribery to get us shorter visits to the Foreign Registration Office. That tedious piece of bureaucracy is one process not worth waiting for.

24. "Religious Pondering" by Anonymous

The 14-minute trailer for the film <u>Innocence of Muslims</u> portrays Mohammad raping a girl and shows his followers torturing an old woman and practicing extortion. In September 2012, this film sparked riots all across the Muslim world, causing dozens of deaths, including that of US Ambassador to Libya Christopher Stevens. It follows a growing trend of religious extremism capturing global attention, ranging from Pakistan's blasphemy laws to Terry Jones' plans to burn the Qur'an.

With the omnipresent nature of the media, which has recently been amplified by social media, marginal extremist groups get large amounts of exposure. Previously unnoticed fundamentalist actions now spark severe reactions across the globe, furthering the polarization of the world's major religions. The problem is not that the messages of these minority groups are becoming more radical, but that people everywhere now have access to them. We need to harness this ease of communication in order to promote understanding rather than hate.

I went to a Lycée Français in San Francisco and have been bilingual since the age of three. This dual exposure to the French and American cultures made me thirst for more, and thus was born my keen interest in languages. In the summer after sophomore year, I began an intensive Arabic course, which I pursued throughout junior year. I chose Arabic because it is both beautiful and, due to the growing instability in the Muslim world, topical. When I came to India, I no longer had access to an Arabic class, but I will definitely continue these studies at the undergraduate level.

The need for open and harmonious communication between the Western and Muslim worlds is apparent as the gap between the two widens due to actions of extremist groups. Engagement is required on all levels, including the educational, political, and religious fronts. I believe that much impact can be made with education through which religious and cultural tolerance can be fostered from a young age. This view is one of the reasons I chose to go to a United World College (UWC). Unfortunately, the Arab world is one place in which the UWC movement currently has quite a small reach. Thus, UWC is effectively fostering a spirit of cooperation among students from many countries while largely leaving out the Islamic nations.

Having complete confidence in education as a way to bring people together is, I recognize, a naïve view to hold. Achieving this harmony will be a difficult and lengthy process. Furthermore, as

Innocence of Muslims has demonstrated, a marginal viewpoint can have an extremely detrimental effect to the cause. Nevertheless, resolving the issue of growing polarization is an important goal, as international cooperation is required for finding solutions to global issues such as overpopulation and the depletion of natural resources. Thus, though I recognize the many roadblocks, I will involve myself as much as possible in working as part of the global movement to confront these problems.

25. "Symposium" by Anonymous

The alarms sound. The room flashes red. An ambulance screeches in.
"Page Dr. Sartre! There's an emergency! A disaster! ... this man is having an existential crisis!"

"I'm right here.", Sartre calmly replied. "Oh my. This man looks dreadful! Put him on 100ml of proverbs stat and see what happens."

"I did... but his body appears to be rejecting the notion of an omnipotent God as we speak."

"I might have guessed. His blood type is skepticism after all. Hmm. Well, first things first. (casually flipping through the patient's chart)...(to himself): "pervasive loneliness, a sense of purposelessness... he *does* seem to exhibit the symptoms of an existential crisis." (Aloud): He needs control over his life- get him 5mg of morphine. Maybe this wil-"

Patient (defiantly): "No! I shall be under no such religious opiate! Why, Karl Marx *explicitly-*"

Sartre (interrupting, in a hushed tone): "Marx. (concerned): This is something far beyond my imagination. We need...the crisis team-now!"

Patient (screaming): "O what is it to be human?! Why do I even exist?!"

Ahh-Just a typical Saturday night. At Symposium, we student interns diagnose a slew of philosophical issues, ranging from the applicability of Ayn Rand's inspiring individualism in today's world to the implications of transvestite Barbie dolls on society, from the secret pleasures of Abe Lincoln to saucy stories of the Turkish baths. Such talk degenerates into a meaningful revelation as to the nature of reality.

Symposium differs from the skin creams and prattle that dominates every day life. Like food and water, symposium is a basic human need, more fundamental than a "sense of belonging" or a "respect of others" which, in comparison, act as hollow substitutes. Symposium refuses to accept that life is successful "as long as one's happy", nor does it diagnose us with the outdated cures of community, love, or religion. Rather, it is something that, when I do, I *know* that there is nothing else more vital- no brain tumor more pressing. Beyond the simulacra- the soulful music, a lover's embrace, the good life- lies symposium. It knows I'm not a liberal, guitar playing, rubix-cube solving lover. No. These are but the choices I have made within what society has offered me- the sum total of the binary options I've chosen as if life was a survey. Beyond this, beyond our very lives, is where symposium delves.

"Away with the superficial," it cries.

It delves into the human within like (Brown's secret society) delves into the depths of time. Beneath the skin of one's occupation, clothes, and interests, shielded by the protecting ribs of marriage, compliments, and kids, lies the swollen, beating heart of humanity. Symposium does not paint the white elephant grey or beat around the bush. Armed with an x-ray and Kantian essay, Symposium dares to defy- incising through the skin and maneuvering behind the bones, with a sharp battle cry, and a need to know why, it approaches the heart, grabs it by the ventricles, and demands, "Who are you?"

26. "Endless Possibility" by Anonymous

I sold my first radish at the ripe age of 6. I can still picture the speechless expression that resonated from my first customer after tasting it for the first time. No, radish is not a code name for any hard drug and yes, the first customer did happen to be my mother. Anyway, at the age of 6, I started my own company, "KJ and Co." I grew sunflowers that were ready to sell only when they were taller than my sister and sold plums at a cheaper price than in Shaw's Supermarket. I harvested tomatoes redder than Karl Marx and cucumbers greener than Al Gore. I was a businessman who offered goods of only the highest quality, employed older children, and, perhaps most importantly, recognized the importance of deliberation before decision making in this world of limited resources. Whether debating to mow lawns or sell lemonade (of which I did neither, because the market was already saturated with other children) or to buy hundreds of water balloons or invest in a Super Soaker (Super soakers were much more powerful), weighing the costs and benefits became an integral part of my decision making at a very young age, a trend that continues today.

For instance, when I was considering applying to your institution, a flurry of thoughts ran through my mind. Paying your $75 application fee would, I conjecture, deny me a multitude of other alternatives. With that $75...

1. I could have paid for .75% of the entrance fee to the World Series of Poker.

2. I could have gone golfing at the prestigious Coto de Caza Golf Club.

3. I could have gone to the Angels-Yankees Game Last Night—in diamond club. DIAMOND CLUB- that's right behind home plate.

4. I could have bought 33.4 cheeseburgers from In-N-Out Burger.

5. I could have filled up my tank of gas! Okay, maybe not fill it up all the way, but at least enough to drive to the Staples Center for the Jack's Mannequin Concert.

6. I could have exchanged it for 514 Chinese yuan for my MUN trip to Beijing in March.

7. I could have bought Baltic Avenue in Monopoly- with 15 dollars to spare!

8. I could have bought a new pair of Cross Country flats.

9. I could have bought a new amplifier for my guitar.

10. I could have upgraded to first class for our Legislative Lobby
    Day trip to Sacramento.

11. I could have bought NBC's "The Office" seasons 1-3 on
    DVD...again.

12. I could have augmented my movie knowledge by subscribing
    to Netflix for an entire year!

13. I even could have even applied to rival Yale, and saved $10.

But, this essay is not a rant on college fees. Strangely enough, this essay documents a vital learning experience for me. From an early age, I was empowered to do as I please. Earning an income, I dreamed of all that I could do. I could live forever, become president of the universe, or eat all the caterpillars I wanted- as a child, I knew that anything could happen in the future. And, rationally, this makes sense- the future is unpredictable, open to chance, and utterly unknowable to us mere mortals. Tomorrow, astronomers could detect radio signals coming from the Andromeda Galaxy, proving the existence of life on other planets. Tomorrow, a pronounced glitch in the matrix could reveal that that advanced life forms named Zertoks actually control our every move. Tomorrow, the United States government could announce a plan to fully fund science programs in public schools. Tomorrow is a concept that abounds in opportunity. However, unless we buy a new amplifier, commit to consuming 33 cheeseburgers, or invest in a quality Harvard education, all we have is endless possibility.

27. "My Mother" by Javier Gutierrez

Since the age of five, I have lived with my mother, younger brother, and younger sister. My father had left my mother a single parent at the age of twenty. The divorce was very sudden, so my mother did not have time to find a job to support us. In fact, having married at the age of 15, my mother had not worked at all her entire life; she believed my father would always be there for her. When reality kicked in, we were left with hardly any possessions or money. My father had taken as much as he could haul away in a minivan my mother had registered under both of their names, presumably to boost their credit ratings. With only $23 dollars in her pocket, a deck of old cards, and three toddlers, my mother found lodging at my grandmother's house. For over seven years, my family lived in this house until my mother was finally able to save enough money to move.

Today, I live with my mother, younger brother, and younger sister – but things are very different. My mother has earned a master's degree in business administration, at one point owned two homes at once, and holds the position of program coordinator for child services. My mother, once a teenage single parent, succeeded even when the cards were stacked against us. It was no easy feat.

My mother's sacrifices and willpower made it possible. My mother gave up her teenage years and twenties to support me and my family, years my mother could have used to have fun like other people her age. Even when her college and work collided with our school schedules, my mother somehow found the time and energy to do it all. I am deeply grateful for all my mother has done for me and for my family. She has played her cards well.

The more I realize how dire my mother's situation was, the more I realize how tough life can be sometimes. I have learned from my mother than one must not be attached to material goods, for they can vanish in a fleeting moment. My mother has taught me that what really matters in life is one's health and education, for those are harder to take away. Therefore, I always strive to learn more and live to preserve my well-being. Of utmost reverence are my mother's sacrifices. I cannot name a person who would give up the greatest years of their life to give me and my siblings the loving, tender care my mother has shown us. Having been this blessed in my adolescent years, I hope to express my gratitude by serving my family, community, and world to the best of my ability. For this reason, I undertake rigorous academics in hopes of achieving my dream career with the best education I can muster. Thanks to my psychologist mother, I have become deeply interested in the inner workings of the mind and now aim to become a neurologist. Even when I feel the stress getting to me, I hold my ground and burn my way through the work. If I am to really make a difference in this world, I believe, I must be willing to put 110% effort into my work. I constantly work myself so that I may be the best I can be. I do not wish to under-use my mind and abilities. To do so would be a waste of my cards. My mother gave it her all to make sure her children were safe and happy. I should at least be able to give it *my* all to reach my dreams.

To this day, my mother dedicates the majority of her time preserving our success, health, and well-being. When I go out to experience the world for myself, I will always remember that my mother is the only reason why I have my life, education, and happiness. In all my life, I do not know if I can ever fully repay my mother for what she has done. My mother roughed through life with sacrifice and endurance. Through her sacrifice and endurance, I have developed what I feel is an unstoppable willpower. I feel I have a significant, but not yet complete, sense of will that will hopefully carry me through future problems and keep me well-off. I know when sacrifice is necessary and when endurance is called for; I have seen it a hundred times over. Like my mother, I will not let the odds

of the situation discourage me. I have been given my hand from the

start, and now it is up to me to play it right.

28. "Robotics" by Annelie Herrmann

I am familiar with success.

At school, my success is measured numerically and printed into neat little rows of black A's that define me as a dedicated student. At a piano competition, success is largely demonstrated by how many black and white keys I can accurately strike with my fingers. At home, my parents assess me further and exhibit my success to their friends. I thrive in a world of theoretical academia and for eleven years was hesitant to place myself in a situation where failure was even a possibility. I excelled in my classes and did well in the eyes of my teachers, piano instructor, and cross-country coach; why branch out? Why try anything new? I stayed comfortably within walls constructed of grades, assessments, and the approval of adults.

That was until I joined the Robotics team.

For the first time, I was attempting something that wasn't intuitive and didn't come naturally. At my first "build" meeting, surrounded by a group of kids adept at manipulating metal and designing chassis, I distinctly remember thinking I had absolutely no idea what I was doing. I felt incredibly out of place: I couldn't even spell chassis, let alone know what one was or how to go about constructing one. I asked a question of an older member and was told "That's like asking what bread is." I felt inadequate and, for the first time in my life, genuinely stupid. At home in the theoretical world of physics and math, it surprised me how difficult it was to find a place and purpose in this new environment. Each day presented me with a new struggle, a new skill to learn. The biggest surprise to me, however, was how much I *loved* being challenged. I loved that I had to struggle so much to grasp what I was learning. Possessing motivation solely my own, unbounded by grades, teachers, or expectations, I delighted in pouring myself into learning everything I could about robotics. I spent hours at home fiddling around on my laptop with my new CAD program, trying to constrain parts of gearboxes to each other in three-dimensional virtual space. Three times a week, I'd become the subordinate of a more experienced member, something my pride would never have allowed before.

And slowly, oh so slowly, I started to learn.

Every day, I became less insecure. I found the time between piano practice, running, and studying to join in on trips to the General Motors machine shop to learn more about building a robot. From learning my way around the shop to using the water jet, I've grown not only as a robotics student, but away from my initial failure. In a year, I've graduated from "newbie" to Shop Manager, a position in which I ensure the team keeps the shop organized, takes accurate inventory, and brings all the proper equipment to competitions. Additionally, I auditioned and was selected to lead the "Engineering Inspiration" team, a small group that reaches out to the community to inspire young engineers and presents these outreach activities to a panel of judges during competitions. I couldn't believe that my mentors had so much faith in me and my improvement that they asked me to lead such an important part of the team. I finally felt like I belonged.

Robotics opened my eyes to a practical world, a world apart from the theoretical one to which I had become so accustomed. The experience helped me learn to adopt a position of ignorance, and taught me how to overcome it and eventually reach a position of leadership. I learned that the way to success can be found through many routes, and that sometimes a journey of humility, learning, and determination can be especially rewarding. Robotics was the best thing that could have ever happened to me: it knocked me down, and forced me to find a way to get back up.

29. "Piano" by Annelie Herrmann

When I was three, my mother started me in piano lessons. While I may not have appreciated it at the beginning, the fourteen years of lessons and consistent, hour-a-day practicing that followed has made music an integral part of my identity, something I can't imagine living without. I've played in state competitions, sung in state choirs, and even helped direct youth choir groups. I've seen a third-grade girl I mentored hit every note in a performance. While playing piano on vacation, I've cried openly with a total stranger after learning that her father continued to play for her even after forgetting who she was. Each of these experiences has touched me in a unique and powerful way. But this essay is not about playing the piano, singing, or even music; rather, it is about the gifts I've received and the lessons I've learned *through* music - and how I hope to return these gifts in the best way I can.

This summer I participated in a three-week long Biomedical Research Internship at Providence Hospital in Southfield, Michigan. The internship included lectures from medical professionals, lab experience, cadaver dissection, and a research project with a partner culminating in an oral presentation to peers and mentors. My partner, a sophomore at Michigan State, suggested we research Multiple Sclerosis in honor of his father, who had the disease. We pored over medical reference texts in the hospital's library and collaborated after hours via email. The work paid off, and the presentation played to rave reviews.

After the internship ended, however, it dawned on me how little my research had really accomplished in terms of helping anyone, my fundamental motivation for pursuing medicine. While our work was interesting and certainly educational for us, it did not add to the preexisting knowledge of the disease, nor did it actually combat it or make a difference in the lives of people affected. My pride in our research waned into disappointment and a sense of helplessness. But over the next several days, I realized that while I didn't make a world-altering discovery, I *could* play the piano, and it may be possible to impact the world, however slightly, with that gift.

I had previously planned to hold a Senior Concert in August as a celebration of my accomplishments in piano. It was to be a grand affair, complete with printed invitations, a rented recital hall, and a floor-length dress. I had been working up fourteen pieces from memory all summer, even practicing in the chapel of the hospital during those weeks when I was short on time. Fueled by my desire to make a difference, I took my Senior Concert to the next level by turning it into a Benefit Concert for the American Autoimmune Related Disease Association (AARDA). I recorded CDs of the program in advance and offered them at the event in return for donations. Nearly 100 guests attended, donating almost $1,000 for the cause, with donors continuing to contribute on my behalf.

There is much I don't know and much I can't do, but my experiences this summer taught me the importance of finding a way to do the most good I can with the talents I do possess. The last song on my program was "Vienna," by Billy Joel, written after Joel visited his father in the Austrian city and saw an elderly woman cleaning the streets with a broom. In response to his son's inquiry, Joel's father explained that she swept because the task made her feel useful. That simple lesson of basic worth inspired Joel to declare in his song that "Vienna waits for you"; a message to all of us that our best contributions come from patient devotion to a clear cause. The song was a perfect ending to something I had worked so hard to accomplish, but at the same time, a beginning for what I hope to accomplish next. As a senior in high school, playing the piano may be the best way for me to make a difference. But I aspire to one day be the one discovering and creating new treatments, not just the one

raising funds to do so.

30. "One Hundred Arms" by Humphrey Obuobi

Stein, my favorite tree near Michigan State University's library, was truly alive. With his arms outstretched, he reached beyond the plane of his body and cradled all the life around him. Resting in those powerful yet docile branches holds a solid position as the most peaceful, reflective moment of that summer. There, I felt like a detached observer, watching spiders as they weaved through the bark, birds as they chirped to one another, and squirrels as they jumped from branch to branch as if they were traversing into a different region of their world. That's exactly what Stein was - a world all on his own, hosting life and the interactions between living beings. My observations there mirrored what I saw in the world at large; just like the spiders or the birds, people interact with people and atoms interact with atoms. Nature itself can be broken down into those fundamental actions and reactions.

One thousand connections.

It only occurred to me midway through my stay in that tree that I was resting in the branches of a nerve cell. In fact, Stein's captivating form reminded me more with every passing minute of Ramon y Cajal's classic drawings of pyramidal neurons, the same ones that I had come across two summers ago when I began my journey into neuroscience. The likeness was almost startling. Stein's supple branches and limbs were nothing more than the winding projections of dendrites.The imposing trunk may as well have been an axon, though this axon burrowed into the ground instead of a forest of glial cells and fellow neurons.

One billion neurons activated in a rhythmic cascade.

The vast ecosystem that was Stein harbored countless natural interactions, and yet, each individual neuron of my mind has the same capability, only on a microscopic scale. This fascination with the neuron's properties is the same force that drives my curiosity about the brain as a whole. For if the neuron is a world, then the brain is a universe. Mind and space are both vast and difficult to understand as a whole, yet their individual components, like the cells and the stars, are much more comprehensible. Computational models that have been developed can only trace the interactions of small networks of nerve cells or stars. Tracking the release of a neurotransmitter in a neural pathway can only get one as far as a probe analyzing Venus' atmosphere can come close to discovering the key to the universe. Still, these microscopic endeavors are united to form a more complete understanding of a macroscopic entity. The quest to understand the brain is a space race all on its own.

In that tree, I realized for myself that thought is not a linear process. My experiences are not compartmentalized, but rather tied together in a continuum. In my mind, the first time I touched the keys of a piano flows directly to the first time I plucked the strings of a viola. In the same way, each thought, each idea, is tied to the next. I simply build upon what I know and connect the dots to form the new, unique ideas which have shaped my intellectual development. It is no surprise, then, that I see the neuron in Stein; to me, the two resemble the same principle of connection that drives and inspires my train of thought.

After ruminating in Stein's arms for the afternoon, I saw some of my friends coming down the path and climbed down from the heights of his dendritic projections and silently bid him farewell. I greeted the group, and Stephen joked about what I could possibly have been doing in a tree for so long.

"What were you doing up there? Dreaming?"

I smiled. "Nope - just thinking."

31. "Cross Country" by Adam Gilfix

"Faster! Sprint it out," I demand of my exhausted body. I pump my arms and drive my legs. As I cross the finish line, seventeen minutes and three miles lie behind me. This is cross-country in its simplest form: long-distance running. Yet, at its core, cross-country revolves around competition, focus, individual growth and improvement, teamwork, integrity, and fun. For me, it is not just an extracurricular activity. It is a mindset, a way of life. Though we race in the autumn, my Dad reminds me "it is a summer sport played in the fall." I agree, summer preparation is crucial, but cross-country is truly a year-round commitment that has shaped me.

My coaches have had especially meaningful influences on me. My middle school coach, Mr. Beane, helped me evolve from sixth-grade endurance athlete to teenage running enthusiast. Coach Beane tracked every performance, motivating me to set and achieve goals for besting my previous results. In high school, Coach Uttaro's inspirational stories before each race emphasize that cross-country requires a mental edge, the determination to will oneself towards the finish line. I have always had this competitive drive. However, in this sport, I developed stronger resolve, forcing myself to put "mind over matter" and "fight through the pain" to succeed.

Cross-country has also taught me sportsmanship and teamwork. Although opposing runners wish each other good luck, we scarcely acknowledge our adversaries after a meet. As a junior, I advocated my captains' proposal of lining up as a team and shaking our opponents' hands. Now, a captain myself, I have carried on this tradition. Furthermore, following Coach Uttaro's example, I deliver pre-race pump-up speeches, fueling my peers with energy and enthusiasm. Once I have sprinted through the finish, I inevitably lose my voice encouraging my fellow runners. In cross-country, personal and team success depend on cooperating with teammates to push each other to our potentials. Consequently, our "Tomahawks XC" motto, "make the jump," applies to "jumps" of improvement for individuals and the overall group.

When not wearing my Algonquin uniform, the ideals I have learned in cross-country stick with me. I incorporate focus and the will to succeed into other pursuits, from family hikes to physics problems to Scrabble games. Whether tutoring, teaching at Hebrew School, assisting friends in class, or helping my younger siblings with homework, my goal is to motivate others in the same positive manner I use on race day. Likewise, I carried over the importance of collaboration to my summer internships. When this past summer ended, I was particularly saddened to say good-bye to my work "team" with whom I had bonded. In a few weeks, I will undoubtedly be crestfallen at my final cross-country banquet, as I depart from my favorite community. However, I will always remain a cross-country runner at heart, sprinting into the future with a competitive drive, a motivational spirit, and a cooperative nature.

32. "Baseball" by Adam Gilfix

It hit me like a freight train, or, more appropriately, a Boeing 737: I just missed my flight. "My boarding pass says that my flight for Tampa leaves from this gate! Please, can they hold the plane?" I frantically plead with the gate attendant, nearly bursting into tears. "How could this have happened?" It was hard to admit, but I had gotten lost: not lost in the airport, but completely lost and submerged in a sea of data.

This journey began a year earlier, when I read an article from a July 2011 issue of *The New Yorker* about Tampa Bay Rays' outfielder Sam Fuld. Despite being a die-hard Red Sox fan, I felt a connection to this rival, who continually persevered through diabetes. His outgoing personality, hustle, and small stature reminded me of myself. However, our greatest commonality is a mathematical mind with an affinity for baseball statistics. Fuld is not only a player, but also a statistician. Likewise, I spend my free time scrutinizing ESPN stats, and eagerly sharing my findings with friends and family. Recognizing this connection, I emailed Fuld, volunteering to help prove his hypothesis of a correlation between foul balls and batting success. Days later, Sam's reply launched our relationship and my work on his project. I was as ecstatic as when the Sox won the World Series in 2004!

Over the following months, I immersed myself in this opportunity to apply my enthusiasm for baseball and mathematics. I treasured every hour of data collection; well, almost. Many obstacles stood on my path to an effective spreadsheet of all 180,000 plate-appearances from the 2011 MLB season. One such hurdle was a fistfight with Microsoft Excel over auto-formatting on imported data. It "only" took weeks of tinkering to resolve this dispute. Yet, every challenge was a chance to learn, and I embraced each one, gaining experience in Excel, as well as in problem-solving and analytical thinking. Just months after Sam's first e-mail, my new favorite ballplayer and I met to discuss my database. Right off the bat, we hit it off.

Still in the airport, I await the next flight to Tampa to see Sam. My blunder had been to flirt with the departure time by finalizing "just one more analysis" for the internship I had obtained due to my Excel expertise (which earned me the nickname "spreadsheet genius"). "I won't make that mistake again," I think, laughing inwardly at myself. My baseball project comes to mind: errors are opportunities.

Though the data did not ultimately corroborate Sam's theory, we continue to collaborate on the project, determined to uncover correlations and enhance current metrics. For now, the world of baseball is the perfect environment to engage my passion for mathematics and data. However, I eagerly anticipate other opportunities, in college and beyond, to implement my analytical skills. I cannot wait to build relationships with classmates and professors and lose myself in my studies; though not so lost that I miss an exam, or worse, a flight.

33. "FOWL" by Sofia Samutin

Turn off a narrow road on to a gravel driveway. Follow the drive until you reach an old tobacco barn, about a mile from the last traces of civilization. Welcome to my grandmother's certified organic farm and the site of my successful, sustainable poultry business *FOWL.*

This is the road I drive down everyday, and the route a group of Iraqi teenagers took when they came to visit the farm and talk to a peer about the entrepreneurial process. This past summer, a group of Iraqi teenagers were chosen to participate in a selective program put on jointly by the U.S. State Department and the World Affairs Council. They were brought to the United States to learn about democracy, leadership, and entrepreneurship. One of the directors at the Word Affairs Council saw an episode of Jean West's Medical Digest, in which I was interviewed about starting and running my business and the importance and my passion for eating local, organic food. The director contacted me and asked if I would be interested in meeting with the group to share my experience.

That day was a moment of great cultural awareness. My world had already been expanded when I moved from Chicago to my grandmother's farm in rural Kentucky. But as I talked with these boys and girls that were from halfway across the world, and had their roots in a starkly different culture, I realized how much I still have to learn about people and the world.

When they first arrived, I welcomed them with a tray of deviled eggs. The significance was to welcome them to American culture with a quintessential dish, as well to illustrate a popular marketing tool for food-based startups. While they were hesitant to try such a different food, they were eager to learn about my entrepreneurial adventure. They asked me about the struggles I had experienced in starting my business. I told them about temporarily living without running water or electricity, rejection by potential retail clients, and the emotional and financial hardship of losing over half my flock of baby turkeys to a flash flood. I encouraged them to use their age to their advantage and always follow their passion: this helps any business succeed through the tough times. I also counseled them on doing their market research, such as I did when I went around Louisville interviewing chefs and purchasing managers to understand the concept of supply and demand for food products.

They were rather shy to share their ideas, and one young man explained that my success was both daunting and inspiring. I realized that I had the opportunity to make other people my age, from a totally different culture, feel that they had the power to make their ideas and passions a reality. I encouraged them to share: I was amazed how many had goals that revolved around health, women's education, and recreation for children. I was surprised and curious and they explained about the rigid, boring lifestyle of girls, how young people had little to do besides homework or get into trouble, and that knowledge of proper health procedures was poor. This is a major juxtaposition to the culture of the United States and was an eye opener. It made me realize how lucky I was, even compared with my personal struggles, to live here with all the possibilities and opportunities available. In encouraging these peer entrepreneurs, I realized that having a

passion and interest and sharing these with others will make one successful and happy.

These young men and women are the future leaders of their country, with concerns for the welfare of their individual towns and people of their state. Their desire to do good and follow their passions has inspired me to join their ranks and to be a leader in my community and country by following my passions that will hopefully benefit and positively impact the world.

34. "Secrets to Success" by Anonymous

My dad maintains that there are four secrets to academic success: get a good night's sleep, sit in the front row, eat a good breakfast, and never miss a class. I've done my best, but I've missed my fair share of school for swim meets, and I rarely eat breakfast. My dad's secrets to success work to a point, but I have added my own secret, one that doesn't just apply to school: list-making.

I have lists for everything. Yellow legal pads pile up on my desk and bedside table, filled with lists: to-do lists: short term and long term, lists of books I have read, lists of books I want to read, movie lists, song lists, potential future career lists, lists of New Year's Resolutions, lists of places to visit, lists of possible senior projects. Completing a challenging task is made all the more satisfying by getting to cross it off a list.

At the beginning of every semester and swim season, I write a list of goals. My goals, though ambitious, are like my typical everyday to-do list in that they are achievable and something I strive towards everyday. When I don't achieve something at first, I don't give up. I copy the goal down onto a new, promising, piece of yellow ruled paper where it awaits my next attempt. My primary goal of last year was to make the Olympic Trials in the 100 Backstroke. It was at the top of all my lists. My mind was constantly occupied with the image of the blue ink on bright yellow paper and the picture on my desk of the colossal stadium where Trials were to be held. I came within a tenth of a second of that ambition, but Trials were last June, and I was at home watching them on TV. Now "make Olympic Trials" is on the top of a newer, crisper list, and I know I will be there in four years.

My lists aren't always serious and they help me maintain a good balance in my life. Writing something on a list is what compels me to plan family trips, hikes, and activities with my friends. Hiking Mt. Katahdin with my siblings was on my "Things to Do This Summer" list, along with a bike ride from Massachusetts to New Hampshire with my best friend. These trips would not have happened if they had not been on my list. Other lists remind me to inbox old friends on Facebook or finish watching Season One of Friday Night Lights.

In college, I will continue to have lists for everything. Whether homework assignments, organizational tasks, or responsibilities for swimming, I will write down everything that I need to accomplish. But after a few weeks on campus I will also have lists of the best places to study and best burritos near my dorm, and lists of new friends to make and school clubs to join. And if it's on my list, I won't stop until I can cross it off.

35. "Delicacy of Life" by Melinda Wang

I picked up my first stirring spoon when I was barely taller than the range oven. Standing on a wooden stool and quaveringly gripping the metal handle of the heavy pan, I first attempted to cook in the hope of easing the burdens of my parents' busy lives. I began with simple dishes such as scrambled eggs and salads, and gradually proceeded to more complex cuisines, such as stir-frying. At the time the complexity did not seem challenging at all – simply cutting the vegetables into pieces, dropping all the chopped ingredients into the pan, stirring, and adding the prescribed amount of spices. I didn't know, however, that cooking is not a miracle. On my first try, with much difficulty, I succeeded in producing an overly bland mix of unevenly cut vegetables covered with soot. On my next attempt, the pieces were uniform, but the bitterness of the soot still permeated my tongue. When I finally corrected my previous mistakes, the spices turned out to be too stimulating. In every instance, the dish was unpalatable.

Undiscouraged by my attempt at cooking, I became relentless. I kept trying until, one day, I realized that crafting a tasteful dish would require effort in all aspects of cooking: chopping vegetables into unvarying pieces, preventing burning or undercooking, and adding the perfect blend of flavoring. Even if one aspect were to fail, the entire design would crumble. Understanding this, I attempted to amend each process meticulously. After a series of successful dishes, my enthusiasm in cooking skyrocketed, as I plunged deeper into the beautiful art of delicacy.

I gathered that this concept of cooking also applied to life in general. Living a fulfilling life mainly consists of aspiring toward our career goals, taking on family responsibilities, and cultivating healthy relationships with friends. Similar to cooking a perfect dish, achieving a meaningful, successful
life demands constant attention to every important aspect of life. Too often in our society, many people define success in life as accomplishments in their careers; thus, they only concern themselves with professional pursuits and neglect other significant aspects, rendering their lives empty of personal connections with others. The lack of such crucial flavors can only add blandness and monotony to an otherwise wonderful life.

Keeping this in mind, I have strived to extend care to all aspects of my life. Although my parents and I are inundated with work, we try our best to share dinner time every day and contribute as much as we can to routine housework. While keeping a good academic standing, I also maintain loving relationships with all my friends; we provide each other academic, emotional, and mental support. During my afterschool hours, I explore various ways to contribute to my school and community, through volunteering and joining extracurricular organizations. Now, armed with the skills to enrich my life and nourish my morale, I can confront life audaciously, and feast on its blessings with my own delicious food.

36. "Diversity" by Karen Maldonado

When I first came to this country, I knew not a word of English. My mother's diligent (and successful) efforts to teach me to read since birth suddenly dissolved in the face of American preschoolers who could not understand my Spanish. The situation was simple to this teary-eyed toddler: walls, in the form of language and cultural barriers, defined my new American life. The walls of our home in Mexico City were the color of maize, not the dingy gray of our Houston apartment. Yet as most children do, I quickly grew fluent in the new language. Still the grayness of the walls persisted.

I built new walls: virtual borders between my heritage and my assimilated persona. By grade school, I barely spoke Spanish at all; upon reflection, this past accomplishment is now a heavy regret. My nationality became a novelty: my birthplace was show-and-tell trivia. And so the remarks began: "But you don't *look* Mexican," is a statement I have heard too many times. All my life others have taken it upon themselves to categorize my identity.

In favor of acceptance, I settled into my ambiguity comfortably. I denied my minority status to accommodate others. It seemed that whenever society acknowledged my race, it acted against me. For years, I straightened my thick wavy hair to fit in with other school girls. In high school, classmates disregarded my opinion in a debate on affirmative action after labeling my immigrant status a bias. By rejecting my own identity I became a gray area, like the musty walls of the apartment I so hated as a child.

It was when the questioning of my appearance evolved that things changed: "It's okay, because you *look white*." Delivered as a compliment by an acquaintance, this twisted assurance of racial mislabeling frankly disturbed me. I questioned the society that encouraged me to assimilate, not to an American standard, I had discovered, but a white standard. This one well-intended but offensive racial remark catalyzed my interest in social justice and diversity education. I have a tendency to dive head-first into new interests, so I took advantage of every opportunity I could to learn more about social justice. I joined my school's Student Diversity Committee and attended the Student Diversity Leadership Conference in both 2011 and 2012. Out of continuous research and discussion, I developed an illuminating insight into both myself and the life I choose to live. What began as an internal fight to accept and take pride in my racial identity evolved into an ardent passion to celebrate diversity in the world around me.

I still catch glances of that little girl who refused to speak Spanish, her awkward straightened hair hanging at her shoulders. She will always be a part of me. Yet, through education and passion, I have found both growth and self-realization. I am Latina; I have faced the struggles of a Hispanic immigrant, and I now embrace my Mexican culture (and hair) wholeheartedly. I am not a novelty; I am not here to show and tell. There is still work to be done for both myself and others. Through further involvement with social justice and diversity education, perhaps I can help another little immigrant girl tear down her own walls. I intend to live proudly as I am and encourage others to do the same. Walls of oppression, of injustice, still exist all around us. In knowing them firsthand, I no longer fear them. Re-imagining my perceptions of my own barriers lead me to empowerment and self-realization. My journey, though arduous, and only in its beginning, has already led me beyond what I could have imagined and shown me a passion for celebrating personal identity.

37. "My Bike" by Anonymous

10 alarm clocks go off simultaneously at 5:17pm- I groan as I force myself to get off the couch and snap out of the comfort of my 15 minutes powernap. I race down the apartment's stairway and hop onto my bike. As I peddle ferociously for 40 minutes up and down a series of hills, I listened to the *KWANK-KWANK* discordance emitting from my bike, indicating that I am perhaps a little too big for the rusty medium sized bike. When I finally reach my destination, a smiling 12 year old boy opens the door and yells "HI BRADLEY!", handing me a piece of paper on which his mother has listed his homework and tests. I greet his grandmother as I glance down the seemingly interminable list- this is going to be a long 2 hours.

At 8:00 pm, I again lift myself onto the bike, this time my brain more tiring from the boy's screaming, my fingers more weary from writing pages of notes, my mouth drier from my constant explanations. The boy's grandmother, perhaps unwilling to distract herself from the TV's soap opera, shoves 20 dollars into my fist without saying a word. As I mutter "Thank you" and peddle away from the boy's driveway, the boy screams "SEE YOU TOMORROW BRADLEY!"

When I reach home at 8:50pm, my mother is standing in the kitchen cooking dinner. Taking off my sweat-soaked T-shirt, I release my fist and drop the 20 dollars on the messy living room table. My mother's eyes meet mine as she saw my return. Then I realize her eyes were unusually watery; embarrassed, I turned away. When she speaks again, it was with her usual warmness: "Thank you". "No problem, I am man of the house after all" I reply.

38. "Immigrant" by Lisette Candia Diaz

Disclaimer: My essay was written and submitted before DACA and it is important to understand this in order to understand the context of the essay.

The sound of running water echoed off the walls of the confined airplane bathroom. My pigtails shook as the plane entered a rough patch of turbulence. Mr. Teddy Bear's hat fell to the ground.

" Why are you wetting that paper mommy?"

"Shhh mi Niña, I'm doing this for us, okay baby, so we can have a better future," She whispered. *"Now when we get there, don't speak to anybody ok? Don't make eye contact with anyone and if anyone asks say you don't speak English?"* she said.

"Si mama, I won't say anything"

My parents decided to immigrate to America in 1999, bringing with them, the same hopes and dreams as the millions of immigrants before them; a better present, a better future, all in attempt to bury their previous mistakes. . I guess they never realised that by wanting to create a better life for themselves, they severely limited my own.

I've lived in the U.S for 12 years. I have more American friends than Spanish friends. I've taken AP classes since they came available to me and yet I still get the same question; *"Wait so you're not from here*?" I don't have an accent, I am often confused for Caucasian, *"But you're so smart!"* I have two eyes and a nose, and am unfortunately plagued with the same insecurities as like the typical teenage girl, *"Do they have, like, a lot of chilli in Chile?"* I mourned the losses of 9/11, I rejoiced in the capture of Osama Bin Laden, I say the pledge of allegiance every morning, but I cannot leave the country to see family nor can I drive like the rest of my peers I grew up with. I am not an American citizen.

"Bonjour classe, It's the moment you've all been waiting for; the trip to France!"

I paled considerably when I heard that, knowing that, despite maintaining one of the highest grades in my French class, I would not be able to go. I looked at the brochure and couldn't help but feel angry at the implications of my situation.

" So Lisette, do you think you're going on the France Trip?" My teacher asked.

"Well, I have to speak with my parents first, but I'll definitely look into it!"

"Good, I hope you come"

"Me too"

I'm nearly 18 years old and I don't have my learner's permit, I don't have my license. *"Aren't you 16 already? Why don't you have your permit?"* I've lied on countless occasions to my friends, to my teachers. *"I'll get it when I have time, I'm really busy right now…"*

But why can't I drive? Why can't I go to France with my French class? Why should I miss out on the opportunity of attending a good university when I worked harder than my American counterparts? I'm in AP English Literature scoring higher than people who are native speakers.

I may not be an American Citizen, but I deserve the opportunity to study at a prestigious university; I've worked hard. I've had to face situations none of my classmates have never even thought about. I've lived in fear for the majority of my life. Hearing stories of deported immigrants who've done nothing more than try to raise their kids in an environment that doesn't involve poverty. But I'm still fighting.

> *"mi nina escuchame, we'll be okay, the laws will change and*
> *we will be able to do everything, just like everyone else"*
> *"ok mami, yo te creo, I believe you"*

My pigtails shook as I bounced into that classroom all those years ago. My name is Lisette Candia, I am an undocumented immigrant but I am an American.

39. "Hurricane Season" by kat baus

I was always terrified of weather. My fear was a storm itself, brewing off the coast of my mind and rushing in with terrible force; just the sight of thunderclouds or evacuation route signs set my teeth on edge. After Katrina—after evacuating, after seeing the carnage on the news from Memphis and Baton Rouge, after showering in friends' gutted basements for their hot water—I thought the fear was gone. Then Gustav arrived. I was older, in a new school, with a boyfriend of almost a year, but I was petrified. I spent the sixteen-hour drive with my iPod on full volume against the strained sound of the voices on the radio. The levees weren't strong enough, they said. This could be the end.

The weekend was a blur punctuated by the static crackle of my boyfriend's voice on the phone. He asked me if I had tried praying. "I don't know how," I told him. I was raised in a lesbian family; my mother went to Unitarian church, but I had left it behind several years earlier. Now, asked to pray, I felt lost. He directed me to a book of Catholic prayers I'd borrowed out of curiosity. Inside it was tucked an unevenly-folded piece of blue paper and a string of cheap plastic beads, also blue, from which dangled a small, imperfect crucifix. "Just give it a try," he said. "For me. I gotta go."

My sign of the cross was shaky, my words faltering, but they grew in strength and certainty as I went on. It became a nightly routine. There was something in the simplicity of those prayers, in the feel of the beads between my thumb and finger, that held me. A sort of stillness.

I began to join my boyfriend at church and soon went more often than he. After a few months, I told my mother I wanted to get baptized. She looked appalled. The church was corrupt, she said; it ostracized gays and denied people's basic rights—how could I believe in that? I couldn't answer her. I couldn't answer my friends, either. They called me a sellout; they didn't know who I was. Neither, I realized, did I. Though at first I was outraged at them for judging me, I came to see that I had judged them just as harshly. I had exploded over their political opinions, scolded my friends for partying, and constantly fought my mother's rules—and I was angry with them for doing just the same.

I wish I could say I fixed things then, but I didn't. I took religious classes for six months and was baptized at Easter. After another six months, my relationship fell apart. It was junior year; I was drowning, dragged down by seven classes—five of them A.P.—and I had driven off anyone who might have thrown me a rope. Nights I stayed up working. Lunches I spent mostly alone.

Then, just before I gave up, faith saved me—not faith in principles, but in people. Sarah was the friend with whom I had fought most bitterly, but she pulled me back to the surface, letting me vent my frustrations and reminding me that I wasn't alone. Gradually, I found my place again. With practice, I learned how to balance my work and ended the year with straight A's and solid test scores. I learned to communicate. I made new friends, healed wounds with old ones and with my family, and reconciled my fledgling faith with my LGBT heritage and identity, becoming president of my school's Gay/Straight Alliance. Most importantly, I learned respect. I learned that storms can strike when we least expect them to, shaking our foundations and flooding us with fear, and that even the strongest swimmer cannot tread water forever. I learned that we cannot survive by going it alone; that we must offer our hands to those who are struggling; that we must make peace— for winds change, and we will all need compassion when the storm is at our door.

40. "Iowans" by kat baus

Rather than slink off to our rooms, we spent Friday night in the lobby, our suitcases piled by the wall, the couches shoved together into makeshift beds, blankets strewn over every surface, until finally each of us gathered his belongings and left. The last week had passed in an instant, and though we were exhausted, none of us wanted it to end.

There were sixteen of us in the lobby, fifty sleeping upstairs, and another batch of sixty-six scattered around the world, waiting to replace us the next week. We had been chosen from a pool of nearly five hundred applicants for the Iowa Young Writers' Studio, a program for aspiring teenage authors at the University of Iowa. My two-week experience there has meant more to me than any other in my thirteen years of schooling.

After drooling over the studio's course descriptions, I chose a poetry class taught by Mary Hickman which consisted of seminars three mornings a week and workshops every afternoon. Mary—I was initially hesitant to call the faculty by their first names, but I came to cherish that reminder that they considered us friends as well as students—had compiled a course packet that included everything from Sappho's confessions of love to Tao Lin's absurd and profound *cognitive behavioral therapy*, and she challenged us with each new set of poems: to write sonnets after Shakespeare and autobiographies after Frank O'Hara, to experiment with Oulipian constraints and marathon hundred-line collective poems. Each night we read selections by two or three students and prepared critiques, which we shared and debated in workshop. The first to lay my work on the cutting board, I was unnerved by my classmates' insights and suffered some heavy blows to my ego, but as I listened to their critiques and produced my own I grew more confident in my understanding and firmer in my revisions. As we became more comfortable, our workshops stretched longer and longer into each afternoon. No one wanted to break the perfect circle we made sitting in the grass outside the lecture hall.

Iowa extended far beyond our small classes. There were nightly readings by authors who shared not only their work but also the experiences that had shaped them and the thoughts they tried to convey. Mary read her own works-in-progress and introduced us to her writer friends, who spoke to us not as children but as colleagues, even asking for criticism. Twice a week, we embarked on "Missions Inscribable," each led by a different teacher. One brought my group to the university radio station to tell stories from our lives.

A boy choked as he mourned relatives killed in a car crash on the other side of the world, another as he told how a friend's father had called in sick to work at the World Trade Center the morning of the bombings. I was embarrassed when my turn came—all I could think of was returning home after Hurricane Katrina—but as I spoke, I found myself crying, and when I stepped down from the microphone, so were the kids who hugged me.

We didn't even know each other's names, but within a few days we became old friends. We spent every moment together, playing ninja, exploring Iowa City, howling over bad fanfiction and adapting it into outlandish skits. One night we sneaked into a dark classroom, lit candles, and took turns reading aloud from a book of short stories by Oates, enjoying the simple sounds of her words and the comfort of each other's company. The adults joined us sometimes—bowling, prowling used bookstores, terrifying us with a prank at a nearby cemetery—but the bond we shared was special, just for us.

In the following weeks we joked that nothing felt the same "in the real world." Coming home was like stepping into a bath of ice, shocking and uncomfortable. With time, of course, I readjusted to life, my passion faltered in the face of schoolwork and college deadlines, and Iowa seemed distant, almost dreamlike—but I have held on fiercely to its memory. I am still in touch with more than forty of my fellow Iowans, and have so far managed to reconnect with two. They have proven to be some of my truest friends. The time I spent with them has taught me not only how to be a better writer but also how to be a better individual, and I can only hope that, as I continue to learn, they will continue to inspire me.

41. "Bras and Stars" by My Ngoc

I remember the first time I wore a bra. I came home from school in the fifth grade, and my mom handed me a white cloth to put on beneath my shirt. "You're a big girl now," she said, "You need to wear this." From that moment on, my life was forever changed.

That same year, I was taught that the sun would someday die, and I, feeling the pressure of the contraption beneath my shirt, realized that my childhood, too, would eventually dissipate just like the sun.

The first bra paved way for a second, and then a third, and then, by the fourth bra I had advanced to the Lady Type, the ones that my mom wore.

With every new bra, I cast away the former. Somewhere in the dark abyss of my closet, there is a heap of abandoned bras, tiny, worn-out filaments that had once shone so brightly in their days of use, but had faded away into old, neglected remnants of days long gone. They sit against a corner of the universe and gather dust like dead stars— without life, without luster, without vigor.

With every new bra, I felt the unmerciful hand of change push me further down a path with which I had no return. The bras no longer had the simplicity of the first; they came equipped with more folds and stitches and frills and patterns that were designed to counteract the growing complexity of my responsibilities.

Sometimes, when I found myself too big for the current one, I was either unable to or unwilling to get another because of the implications behind the transition—if every new bra meant the death of another star, then the adult world was nothing to me but a lifetime of darkness. I tried so hard not to kill any more stars, but my resistance was not enough, and I found myself adding layer after layer to the ever-increasing pile of bras. With this mindset, I prepared myself for the end, for the moment in which my entire universe would be engulfed by the black hole forming in my closet.

But I was saved.

I learned that life does not occur linearly, but in cycles: New stars can arise from the ashes of former ones, and the darkness of death is replenished by the light of birth. Thus, what is created is only a reinterpretation of the past in a form that is fitted for the present. In wearing a new bra, I was not casting away my old self but reorienting myself to accommodate to changing times.

Change, as overwhelming as it feels, is only natural—the pile of bras will only get bigger. Though it is hard to accept the existence of the bra in my life, I realize that I cannot live without it, for, as we grow older, things tend to droop more easily, and there is nothing more reliable than a bra to give us the inner support necessary to have a firm hold on life.

42. "The Alarm Clock" by My Ngoc

I have never liked alarm clocks. I want to sleep, and there is nothing more annoying than the incessant burst of noise that tears me away from my dreams. But to those who are young, those who have never been ripped away from their dreams, those who have never heard the harsh resonance of the siren, those who have never had to feel the dread of reaching the finish line unexpectedly, time is dimensionless.

But I am not young anymore.

I have always told myself that I have time. What's the rush? I still have four more years to decide my major, one more year to pick a college, thirty more minutes of sleep until I would have to run for the bus. There was either no time left or all the time in the world, and because I was young, I always pictured in my mind the latter. But over and over again, my vision would contradict with reality, and by now I understand that I can no longer deny the existence of the alarm clock in my life.

It came slowly at first, creeping in with such subtlety that I did not even know it was there. I was taking the SAT at the time, inching my way through the test, analyzing each answer choice and thinking of how great my scores would be when suddenly the proctor stood up and announced that we had five minutes left to finish. I looked down and saw that I had barely made it to the halfway mark.

I felt like crying. I did not realize how little I had accomplished until it was all over. But back then I was still young, and the consequences were not of enough magnitude for me to take them seriously. After all, I only lost a fourth of a point for each wrong answer. Surely a few skimpy numbers would not stop *me* from going to college.

For a while nothing happened. The test results from the first SAT came back, and they were good enough that I would not have to do a retake. The world resumed its normal pace, and I, too, slid back into the cadences and rhythms of my old life. I relaxed, thinking I would never have to deal with that alarm clock again until one day, it came back to visit me, bringing with it a dread like that which comes upon the realization that the monster under the bed did not disappear but was actually waiting patiently in the closet. This time, it was intent on teaching me the lesson I never learned. This time I would *have* to take it seriously, for this time, it was not SAT points I would risk losing but the very core and creator of my existence—my mom.

I am sleeping one night when noises start to settle on the surface of my consciousness. I hear belching noises, wails of pain. It is four in the morning though, so I think it is just my mind distorting the wind outside. I fall back asleep thinking that they would stop, but the noises keep on crawling on the peripheral of my senses, and half an hour later I wake up again to find them echoing even louder inside my head. Someone is throwing up downstairs, and from what I hear, it is serious. I scramble out of bed and down the stairs and am greeted by the sight of my mom sprawled on the floor.

My dad and my sister are already there, but no one utters a noise except Mom, who shrieks, "Dao bung, dao qua, troi oi DAO QUA!" *My stomach hurts, it hurts, oh god it HURTS!*

The next few minutes pass by in a blur. My sister tells me to stay home. "Mom'll be okay," she says, "Don't worry about it and go to school." They carry her out to the car, close the doors, and speed off. I stand in the driveway and watch the headlights disappear, and I continue to stay fixed to the pavement as the cold slowly bites its way into my body, freezing up every drop of blood as it inched its way to the end of each and every capillary.

Otherwise, there are few remnants of that night—only the confusion, the bewilderment in my dad's eyes, the limpness of my mom's body and the painful agony in her moans. Most of all, I remember seeing an alarm standing on top of my mom's belly, the same one that had once stood on my shoulders. "Look who's back," it said, and started to jump up and down, making my mom scream with every landing. I tried so hard to kick it away, but I could not budge; I could only stand there and watch it destroy my mom, whose agonizing moans interlaced whatever memories I had left of the night.

When I go back inside the clock answers me with five dismal rings, and I battle the harshness of its droll by cleaning up the mess on the floor. Afterwards I take a long shower, make breakfast, and sit at the table for a long time staring at the same spot. The lemon-fresh hardwood cleaner I used smells bitter and pungent, just like bile, and I leave for school thinking that my sister had lied to me.

Eight restless hours later, I visit Mom with my sister, who brings along a bouquet of yellow chrysanthemums. They are my mom's favorite flowers, and for that I despised them. During the whole entire ride they only gaze up at me with mocking grins, flashing me with a happiness that only contrasts so despairingly with the hopelessness I feel inside—I only see them decorating Mom's funeral. Any drops of hope had long ago frozen within me. Yet, when

I finally see my mom on the hospital bed, when she smiles back with all the liveliness and warmth I so love, the smirks turn to smiles, and the ice within my body melts into tears, sliding down my cheeks and fall onto the flower petals. I put the chrysanthemums next to the window and let the sun splash puddles of light over the sweet drops of perspiration covering the petals.

The doctors never found out what caused the stomach pains. At first they thought there was an obstruction in her pancreas, which happens when a kidney stone strays off and gets stuck in the tubing, but the ultrasounds revealed nothing of the sort. Then they thought it was high cholesterol, which would have made her pancreas highly overactive, but, again, nothing. After weeks and weeks of analyzing and reanalyzing, they gave up and blamed it on stress.

I knew what it was, though. I was the only one who knew, but I did not say a word because I knew no one would believe me—it was the alarm clock, and it had come to give me the retake I never took.

I never got back my scores from the final retake, and I suppose I never will, for this is a test that never ends, and because there is no ending, everybody passes and everybody fails. Time is the result of constant change, so as long as we are subject to its dimensions, we must all face the ultimate test of lowering the substance that seeps out from time's ever moving feet, entropy, which incorporates itself into our lives as the weeds of death, decay, and disease. I can feel the minutes sliding through my body like an army of stray electrons, and I realize their value when I think of my neighbor, who died suddenly of kidney failure and lay dead in his house for three days until his son discovered whatever remained of his corpse. I can only be grateful for each passing second, each fleeting hour. Time runs, and it moves faster than I can bubble in the answers, and though I cannot retake this test, all I can do is to prepare to face the next examination and learn to use the alarm clock—even if snoozing is no longer an option.

43. "How to Get Out of a Bunk Bed" by Jiwei Sun

I was stuck in a bunk bed. I was on the top bunk and I was supposed to be lining up outside the door with the other campers. But I was stuck. I had no idea how to get down. *Maybe I could jump down? It might hurt, however, and I don't want to start camp off with a sprained ankle.* My mind raced for ideas on how to get down without embarrassing myself too much. *What if I put one foot on the bunk below me, then lowered myself down? Dang it, I can't reach the bottom bunk.* I looked over and saw most of the campers were already out the door. *All the campers are gonna think I'm weird for taking so long to get down. Gosh, it's going to be so embarrassing.* Time was running out. I had to do something, quickly. I took a deep breath, and I jumped.

And I landed. And it didn't hurt. I had become so paralyzed with worry over what the others would think about me that I had temporarily forgotten how to get off a bunk bed. This has long been a problem of mine. No, not forgetting how to get off bunk beds. Rather, I've always tried to get everyone to have a good impression of me. I wanted to please everyone and would hate for anyone to dislike me or to find me annoying or weird. Sometimes, this negatively affects me. Imagine how silly I must have looked, sitting on the top bunk, looking back and forth between the ground and the door, contemplating whether or not I should jump down as if it were a life or death situation.

As I look back to my time at Boys State camp, I now realize why I had so much fun. It wasn't like all those times during large-group discussions at school where I kept quiet because I was worried someone might find my answer to be silly. Nor was it like all those times at the dentist's office when I refused to get braces because I naively thought people would laugh at me for wearing them my last year of high school. At Boys State, I was liberated. I didn't worry about how others viewed me. I figured this was almost like a fresh start for me; I was going to meet people I had never met before, and I wanted them to get to know the real me, not some fabricated version of myself. So, I stopped thinking of how I should impress everyone around me and I started to just be myself. Stealing chairs from general assembly, catching the game-winning frisbee toss, playing pranks on other cabins, and even speaking impromptu in front of a crowd of eighty boys -- all with people I had only known for a few days.

Ever since my experience at Boys State, I've begun to believe I can be myself around others. People should like me for who I am. I've become more comfortable around others-- both familiar and unfamiliar -- because I spend less time worrying about how I'm acting and more time just being who I am. As a result, I've been able to speak up in class more often and get braces as a senior. This new way of thinking also helped me enjoy the rest of camp more thoroughly. And by the time the end of camp rolled around, I was jumping out of the top bunk with ease. Maybe once in awhile, I might slip while jumping down. But it's okay. That's just who I am.

44. "Class Discussion" by Lance Katigbak

All I could do was watch. I watched the speakers eloquently voice out their opinions. I watched the professor steer the conversation. Normally, when you come to class without having read the assigned chapter, or any chapter in the book, for that matter, you get lost in the discussion. That's not how I felt then. Though I had no background information about Chapter Two of "Happiness: The Science Behind Your Smile", I absorbed each student's analysis so naturally, it felt like it had been directed towards me.

I was visiting Boston, and my friend Michi had invited me to come to Harvard and attend one of her classes. She said it was called a Freshman Seminar. Aside from the unusual roundtable setup, I noticed that they were not learning about your usual topics in the hard sciences or traditional humanities. They were studying of all things, happiness. Imagine, a class on happiness! I had never encountered anything remotely similar in the past.

After that sneak peek from Harvard, I became curious. I wanted to know what other unconventional topics were offered at such a prestigious university. I thought that all the classes at Harvard would be incredibly difficult to understand, but this experience had eliminated that perception completely.

When I left the class, I began thinking about the things that made me happy. I thought about my family. I thought about my friends. I thought about my charity work in One Million Lights, where we distribute solar-powered lights to residents of off-grid communities. There was an innumerable list of topics under each category that I always thought was purely extracurricular. The opportunity to explore them in an academic setting excited me.

This discovery was a catalyst to a fundamental change in my mindset. My current university focused mainly on rules and hard skills such as logical fallacies and camera operation. Although learning pre-professional skills was important to me, I was now equally interested in the things that I never knew could be connected to academics. I wanted to learn about things like happiness, relationships, and morality. I wondered if there was anything I could take at the University of the Philippines.

When I arrived home, I immediately searched UP's course catalog for those classes. I was disappointed. Unfortunately, UP's pedagogical approach is almost completely pre-professional. At times, it even feels limiting. As the leading state university in a developing country, they are mandated to produce graduates that can contribute to their respective industries right after graduation. While I understand the value behind this approach, I am not fully convinced that it is the right one for me.

I would like to transfer to Harvard because I know that your curriculum will enable me to synthesize both interests—learning about the intricacies of life while developing hard skills in the process. My perception of the real world has expanded beyond UP's career-centric definition. If living is as much a part of the real world as working, then I would very much like to learn about it as well. My undergraduate education is the portal to my future. UP already equipped me with career skills. Now, I want Harvard to teach me about life.

45. "Ready" by Gabriella Germanos

It's been nine months. It's not over yet. My arm tenses in anticipation of the hours of clenching and clutching to come. *I'm not ready*. The sea of people, my people, melts together into one living mass, breathing steadily, rhythmically; somehow we've made it through, raw and weary but hardly defeated. I close my eyes to soothe the pounding beat reverberating through my body. *Gaby, you're ready.* I hear the signal. *You're ready.* I've trained for this moment—I know what I must do: analyze the lasting effects of President Reagan's economic and social policies. With a small smile and a sigh of buoyant relief, I pick up my royal blue pen and watch the dark, College Board-approved ink flow across the page.

For most high schoolers in their junior year, the coming of AP exams spells out torture, a less-than-celebratory culmination of too much time spent taking far too many notes. For me, there are few places where I feel more content than in my school's vaulted gymnasium, my brain stuffed with facts and my desk almost bare. My friends know I'm a diligent student, always prepared for tests, but so are they; what differentiates myself from the others crammed into the room is something I probably won't admit to them, as it always elicits furrowed brows and mouths twisted in confusion.

When I decide to take a leap of faith and begin explaining to someone my bizarre love of AP exams, I point to one particular section of the test that hasn't yet failed to beguile me: the essays. Writing has been a favorite pastime of mine since I was little, and although I can't illuminate a profound reason why argumentative and analytical essays have always given me the warm-and-fuzzies, I do know that spending two hours doing nothing but writing both challenges and calms me. As someone who finds constant stimulation a necessity, I thrive under pressure, finding solace, and often my best ideas, in a time-crunched situation. Of course, after first reading an essay prompt, my heart beats a little faster, and I feel that all-too-familiar sense of trepidation wash over me as I suddenly forget everything I studied. But with a single deep breath and the strangely zen-like process of repeating to myself over and over that yes, I *can* do this, the adrenaline kicks in, and from that point on, I'm in control.

Every aspect of my feelings towards AP essay writing, particularly on the English Literature exam, reveals why I want to explore a career in law. Marking up a text to find evidence satisfies my inner investigator. To prove my point, the performer in me interprets the facts and engages the reader with cogent and poignant arguments like a trial lawyer engages her jury. And no matter how dry or dense the passage (sometimes as difficult to sift through as legal jargon), scrutinizing its subtle nuances can bring to light a brilliant satirical jab or a refreshingly novel perspective, often imparting more wisdom than whatever I used to ace the exam.

Do I stress out before, during, and after AP exams? Absolutely. Do I walk out of the gym feeling exhausted and more than a little apprehensive? You bet. But regardless of the grade I receive, I'm glad I took the exam, as I have proven to myself what I'm capable of, and the boost of confidence I've gained translates to everything else I do: I can hold my trumpet bell high in the air, improvise movement onstage and not care about people judging me, and pour my heart and soul into college application essays without feeling the need to hide any part of me. Having said that,

Hi, I'm Gaby, and I'm the weird, eclectic, totally unique girl who likes taking AP exams. Give me a Queen of the Nerds crown, if you want; just don't forget my royal blue pen.

46. "Senior Year Move" by Anonymous

My first day of senior year didn't quite match the conventional one I had imagined when I began high school. I was in a new school—three times larger than my old one—and I didn't know a single person except for my younger sister. I got lost on my way to every class and had to repeatedly ask for directions. I was in Santa Barbara, California and completely terrified.

I was born and raised in Juneau, Alaska, the third of four children and the daughter of two prominent local doctors. Juneau is a small, isolated—the only way to get there is by plane or boat—and tight-knit community. For me, this was the ideal environment to grow and mature. That being said, I pride myself in being flexible and open to change. Last year, with my full support, my parents applied to an Executive Masters in Public Health program at the University of California: Los Angeles. They were accepted, and our family moved to Santa Barbara in August, arriving less than a week before school started. Though my heart remains in Alaska, I've learned a great deal about the world and myself during the short time I've spent in California.

My father and both of my older brothers graduated from Juneau-Douglas High School and we were well known as a family.

This reputation and Juneau's size gave me a strong sense of responsibility. Starting my freshman year, I immersed myself in most of the available clubs and activities including Student Government, the basketball team and the school newspaper. These were all local pursuits, with strong town support, and I loved seeing the direct impacts a project or an event would have on the population. It felt surreal to walk unknown through a new town and school, and I missed everything that I left behind.

One of the hardest things about moving was saying goodbye to everyone I'd grown up with. I'd known many of my classmates since pre-school, but in Santa Barbara I've had to learn how to meet and befriend strangers. My sister and I had always been close, but now, by necessity, we've become each other's best friends. On days when we're overwhelmed or lonely, we're able to confide and lean on one another. I've realized that no matter how crazy and unpredictable life can get, family is the one constant. With this awareness I've been able to strengthen and reinforce the bonds I have with my other siblings and my parents.

A major change has been having entire classes full of ambitious and driven students. In Juneau, these people existed but they were sparse. Once an oddity, I'm currently surrounded with like-minded people and it has been one of the most stimulating experiences of my life. Deep discussions in class and spontaneously with peers make me contemplate and question my opinions and beliefs. Now, I am more excited than ever about the social and academic environment I will be absorbed in during college.

Fast-forward two months and now I walk through the hallways laughing with friends. We go to sports games on the weekends and I cheer loudly for the "Dons." I've become more involved and familiar with my school. I'm able to give tourists directions to arbitrary locations and know the most efficient routes to drive across town. It's not, and never will be, Alaska, but I've adapted and made it home.

47. "Think Responsibly" by Anonymous

She was blue but not a healthy blue. More like an "I'm not getting enough oxygen" blue. I was squatting next to her in some stranger's dark, dank basement filled with screaming, crying, and histrionic teens. It was pretty clear that none of us knew what to do. And then the girl started to vomit, which was good because that meant she was still alive, but bad too since I was now covered in puke. People were scrambling - trying to find towels, call parents, or just clear out of the house. In the midst of this pandemonium, I finally got it together enough to dial 911. A few of us fought to suppress our panic while the guy on the phone talked us through checking the girl's pulse and counting her breaths until the ambulance arrived.

Although she was all right after having her stomach pumped, I could not escape the guilt that proclaimed that I was partially responsible for her condition: I should have been more diligent, I should have recognized the signs earlier, I should have called the ambulance sooner, and so many other "should"s. That night, I realized my utter disgust at my own helplessness. I discovered that I hated being unable to contribute when a friend was in need. My mom is a doctor. My grandfather is a doctor. I've spent years watching them respond to "Is there a doctor in the house?" and answering countless medical questions at family gatherings. After my frustrated recount of the night, my mom said that while it was noble to embark on a ten-year journey of pre-med-med-intern-resident, perhaps learning CPR now would be of more immediate use.

In order to be better prepared for situations like that and many others, I agreed that it would be beneficial for me to learn at least basic life support. But I figured, why stop at just me? Why not introduce a life support course for students at BB&N? In collaboration with the school nurse, I organized an online course for students with on-campus testing in basic life support. I really did it just to educate myself, but surprisingly, twenty of my peers asked to join me. Now, every semester when I send out a school-wide e-mail, another dozen students receive training. Slowly but surely, we are going from a group of powerless teenagers to a group of responsible adults.

48. "Bolivian" by Anonymous

As a young Bolivian growing up in a the white suburbs of the deep South, I have experienced an upbringing clashing your typical American upbringing intertwined with a variant of Hispanic set of traditions and familial values. Among the typical scholarly objectives of maintaining high GPAs, attaining solid SAT scores, and exhibiting As across transcript, I pride myself in having developed unique goals originating from a truly Hispanic-American spirit. In order to successfully explain the circumstance of my goals, one must understand the complexity of my upbringing.

Immigrating to the U.S. at the age of four already introduced me into a very different culture from which, having come at such a young age, I should have regarded as my only culture; however, my entire family grew up in Bolivia. Thus, I became destined to interlace my original way of life with a new one. As the years passed, I began to comprehend the concepts of hard work, love for one's family, having a zest for life, and a healthy amount of ambition provided by my grandfather who had been CEO of his own shoe factory in Bolivia years before. The sheer amount of dedication he deposited to labor for his family taught me lessons of hard work, treasuring one's home, and prizing one's closest relationships. Many, especially in American culture, tend to overlook how easily family can disappear, but I have an ingrained mentality of keeping close ties with my loved ones for as long as possible.

In addition to comprising the first generation of my family to grow up in the United States, I also endured a severe childhood disease whose bitter years produced an individual who learned to understand the healing power of raw familial love, in spite of the fact that my father left my family at the same time. As my mother's side has always given alms since our beginnings in Bolivia, I too have grown a passion for helping others. This family taught benevolence in conjunction with my profound knowledge of the human body from the years spent in hospitals has helped me develop my ultimate goal of becoming a surgeon.

In accordance with the resolute, ambitious Bolivian-American man I happily embody, my goals only expanded after deciding to enter the medical field. As my years of French studies began at age 13, I fell in love with this close relative of my mother tongue. All those years spent learning about Latin cultures at home suddenly became my passion for learning about European life, customs, language, lifeblood. Then, in my junior year of high school, I further combined my passions for medicine and worldwide cultures. I further enhanced my original goal to include joining a humanitarian organization. I decided that someday I will partake in a medical humanitarian initiative abroad, similar to the efforts of Doctors Without Borders.

How my conditions of goal development reached their apex came about through a series of tumultuous experiences backed by Hispanic teachings laced with what some coincidences, and other would call destiny. My personality and decisions for my future may not have existed had it not been for my kidney disease or the Brady Bunch-like family I call my own, but my fundamental character and goals would always trace back to some fiery traits common to Hispanic culture. I consider myself fortunate to have been raised in an environment where my heritage and personal willpower has certainly helped to burst some budding dreams of mine into charging, resolute aspirations. I take it to mean that my next cultural expansion will only help me in my coming evolution, and hopefully render some tangibility to the things I wish to manifest and become.

49. "My Father" by Muhammed Ors

My earliest memory is of the workshop in my father's picture framing store. For the moment, my father is away. I seize the opportunity to freely explore the room before he returns, noticing a sheet of mirror glass lies on the worktable, waiting to be cut and framed. Quietly, I climb onto it and sit on the mirror. Staring down, I realize my father's smiling face is visible next to mine in the reflection. Looking back on my life, it feels like his smiling face from that day has never left my side.

In 2001, my father sold that store and instead became the landlord of a building, fulfilling a lifelong dream, but at a bad time; growth of local business had stalled with the terror attacks fresh in America's mind. As a Muslim, my father experienced more problems than others finding stable tenants. Because of this, I have seen him disappointed more than happy, but I have also learned more about life than I ever would have otherwise. He is, undoubtedly, the strongest and most influential person in my life. I will forever be grateful to him for opening my eyes to the endless limits of one's own potential.

He has taught me that the deepest satisfaction comes from your own two hands, from sweating and bleeding to complete a necessary project. One such project was the renovation of a derelict apartment in our building, which had become a fire hazard. After prying out a window and breaking apart the surrounding wall, I uncovered large rusted iron bars hanging by fraying rope; these windows still used the outdated pulley-and-weight system. Because of this, we couldn't install new ones without first building from scratch the framework needed for a standard-sized window. Naturally, I began to measure the dimensions of the now gaping hole in the wall so we could properly build new framework. And then, my father did something completely unexpected.

I did not know what true terror was until, at twelve years old, I saw my father freely hanging out of the wall, three stories above the ground, examining bricks on the outside. One second I had the tape measure in hand, the next it was flung across the room and I was screaming deliriously at him to get back inside where it was safe. The terror I felt in that moment will stay with me forever, as a lesson on the lengths one must be willing to go to hold onto one's dreams; if he had not been willing to fix those outer bricks, the renovation would have been incomplete, and the building deemed unsafe.

I have learned from him that, no matter what comes in life, I need to be strong enough to fix the problem. Even when treated like an uneducated foreigner, even when tenants disappeared without paying rent, even when my father was forced to get another job because the income from the building wasn't enough, he persevered and so shall I. It does not matter what the issue is, or where it comes from, because I know I can overcome it. My father has taught me that there are no excuses in life, that, under no circumstances, can I give up on my dreams.

50. "One day I Will" by Muhammed Ors

I distinctly remember the moment in my childhood when I stopped playing with fire trucks, the moment when I stopped thinking "maybe I'll be" and started saying "one day I will." It was a very late night. I was in the car with my father driving home, at the last red light before my street, when a shooting was mentioned on the radio. Normally, I would have been sleeping, but at that moment I was wide awake and my father noticed. He turned to me and paraphrased a verse from the Qur'an that seared itself into my mind: "Whoever kills a person, it is as if he has killed all of mankind, whoever saves a person, it is as if he has saved all of mankind."

When the light changed and he turned away from me, I was left breathless. It was as if a light had changed within my own life and, at ten years old, I understood that I was only a small part of a bigger picture. The tornado of unorganized thoughts that had filled my head seconds before coalesced into a singular, immovable goal: to one day save a life and leave this Earth better than I found it. But, the world had enough doctors *already* doing their best to save lives. It would not mean enough to me to just be another; I would have to go beyond that, I would have to transcend traditional medicine. My difference would be made as the doctor that cured the incurable, the doctor that gave patients second chances that no one else could. I promised myself that, no matter what else the future held, I would find a way to fulfill this dream.

The first step towards doing so came many years later, in Anatomy and Physiology class. My teacher exposed my class to embryonic stem cell research and the ethical debate surrounding it, sparking my interest. Intrigued by the potential, but unsatisfied by the overview, I turned to scientific journals to satisfy my curiosity. I found that embryonic and induced pluripotent stem cells could be differentiated into any type of cell found in the human body, theoretically enabling doctors to grow organs to treat their patients. Stem cell research also provided vital information on how specific genes are expressed, knowledge which could then be used in gene therapy trials, like the one that successfully treated a type of congenital blindness. Reading further, I began to realize the endless possibilities stem cell research promised. When it clicked, my eyes opened wide as a jolt ran down my spine, and, once again, I was left breathless. My mind flashed back to the solemn oath I swore years prior and, suddenly, I knew how to fulfill it: through gene therapy.

Recently, I read in the news about a seven month old baby whose condition causes his blood vessels and skin to progressively harden, resulting in extreme pain when touched. At the top of that article, there was a picture of a smiling and rosy-cheeked baby, covered completely in bruises and lesions. My heart completely shattered when I saw it. This baby lives filled with pain because he was born missing a single gene. He cannot even find solace within his mother's hug, for that would hurt him more. That, to me, is unacceptable. If it has been proven that gene therapy can reverse genetic defects in grown humans, then I believe that conditions like his can be reversed before birth. Reading this article has strengthened my determination, because now I truly see what can be achieved. Traditional medicine can only treat the symptoms; I want to prevent the cause. College will be only the second in a long line of steps, but one day, I will make sure no one has to live a life haunted by genetic disease.

Every year since my thirteenth birthday, during the holy month of Ramadan, I read the entire Qur'an, one surah a night for thirty nights. I have read classics of modernity, such as *All Quiet on the Western Front*, and antiquity, such as *Odyssey*. Yet, no matter what I read, nothing has ever moved me as much as my father's quote. I will never forget the moment I stopped playing with fire trucks, the moment I realized my purpose in life. Because of that conversation, a conversation where he spoke and I understood, I will become a doctor that cures the incurable; I will become a doctor that gives patients second chances before they are even born. I believe wholeheartedly that, when I die, I will leave behind the world better than I found it.

51. "Secrets to Success" by Anonymous

My dad maintains that there are four secrets to academic success: get a good night's sleep, sit in the front row, eat a good breakfast, and never miss a class. I've done my best, but I've missed my fair share of school for swim meets, and I rarely eat breakfast. My dad's secrets to success work to a point, but I have added my own secret, one that doesn't just apply to school: list-making.

I have lists for everything. Yellow legal pads pile up on my desk and bedside table, filled with lists: to-do lists: short term and long term, lists of books I have read, lists of books I want to read, movie lists, song lists, potential future career lists, lists of New Year's Resolutions, lists of places to visit, lists of possible senior projects. Completing a challenging task is made all the more satisfying by getting to cross it off a list.

At the beginning of every semester and swim season, I write a list of goals. My goals, though ambitious, are like my typical everyday to-do list in that they are achievable and something I strive towards everyday. When I don't achieve something at first, I don't give up. I copy the goal down onto a new, promising, piece of yellow ruled paper where it awaits my next attempt. My primary goal of last year was to make the Olympic Trials in the 100 Backstroke. It was at the top of all my lists. My mind was constantly occupied with the image of the blue ink on bright yellow paper and the picture on my desk of the colossal stadium where Trials were to be held. I came within a tenth of a second of that ambition, but Trials were last June, and I was at home watching them on TV. Now "make Olympic Trials" is on the top of a newer, crisper list, and I know I will be there in four years.

My lists aren't always serious and they help me maintain a good balance in my life. Writing something on a list is what compels me to plan family trips, hikes, and activities with my friends. Hiking Mt. Katahdin with my siblings was on my "Things to Do This Summer" list, along with a bike ride from Massachusetts to New Hampshire with my best friend. These trips would not have happened if they had not been on my list. Other lists remind me to inbox old friends on Facebook or finish watching Season One of Friday Night Lights.

In college, I will continue to have lists for everything. Whether homework assignments, organizational tasks, or responsibilities for swimming, I will write down everything that I need to accomplish. But after a few weeks on campus I will also have lists of the best places to study and best burritos near my dorm, and lists of new friends to make and school clubs to join. And if it's on my list, I won't stop until I can cross it off.

52. "Jackass" by Anonymous

If you had told me at the beginning of my junior year that AP US History, the class I had always heard had a daunting amount of reading, would be my favorite class, I probably would have laughed. Now, if you had told me that it would be my class with the most work, then I would have believed you, because it was. However, half asleep on my blue couch where my figure seemed to have worn a permanent spot from the number of hours I spent there, I read some of the most interesting material in my entire high school career. Despite the fact that I was forewarned that attempting to read the whole textbook was impossible, I made it my goal to conquer the thing. The amount of detail that the nightly allotment of reading added to each class transformed history before my eyes. I was able to appreciate the past in a way I never had before, due to anecdotes that hit closer to home than a summary and really made me think about how life became the way it is today. For example, I had always known that each political party had a signature animal, and I knew that they were the elephant and the donkey, but I couldn't remember which one went with which party and didn't know why, exactly, political parties even needed official animals. However, when we learned about Andrew Jackson's presidency, and the fact that he was dubbed "the jackass" by his critics, not only was it humorous, but this fact also helped burn into my brain that the Democratic animal is the donkey. Details like this one really help me to remember facts that would otherwise have to be blindly memorized. In addition, details about specific people affected by tragedies such as the Great Depression or either of the World Wars helped me to appreciate the magnitude of events that happened only decades ago, but previously felt light-years away. AP US History took a lot of work and self-discipline, and I am so glad that I stuck with it, because I will never forget the lessons I learned there.

53. "My Genius Brother" by Anonymous

My brother Jordan is a genius. He was a National Merit Scholar, earned a 4.6 GPA the last quarter of his senior year of high school, was a candidate for the Presidential Scholarship, and now attends Massachusetts Institute of Technology, one of the most prestigious institutions of higher learning in the world. Despite his academic achievements, he is humble, gracious, and helpful to all.

Now it may seem strange that I am recounting so much about someone else in my college essay, but I believe that my brother's success has played a large part in shaping my own. One could argue that without him, I would not be where I am today.

Growing up, being "Jordan's little sister" could sometimes be tough. He was that perfect child that many parents wished was their own, while I was just his younger sister. Throughout lower and middle school, I sought any chance to be better than my brother, even in something as trivial as the quality of our handwriting. We were constantly in competition for grades, and he usually won. In my mind, everything turned into a contest in my desperate attempts to prove my superiority in anything.

Then, when I was in 7th grade, I discovered something new that I loved: sailing. It became "my thing." Jordan didn't sail, and therefore it would be something that I could always have as my own. Little did I know, Jordan would join the high school sailing team the next year. At first, I was devastated. He went on to become one of the best crews on the team in less than a year, and "my thing" was no longer just my own.

Once I moved up into high school, I too joined the team. With the move into higher grades came maturity and a relaxing in our competitive tension. My brother and I actually began sailing together, in the same small boat. We worked hard and became one of the most competitive duos on the team. The funny part of all of this? In our two-person boat, I was the skipper and my older brother was my crew. Though I could possibly have viewed this dynamic as a win on my part and something where I could finally be better than Jordan, I did not, because as I have progressed through high school, "winning" has become less important to me. As my parents have always said, Jordan is the only brother I'll ever have, and that relationship has become more important to me than the constant quest for victory. In fact, he is my best friend and someone with whom I genuinely enjoy spending time; we even own a car together. Though some faint traces of competition still linger between us, they are much more playful and harmless than before.

Looking back, it was silly of me to feel so competitive with everything that Jordan did. Though I used to think of my brother's success as an obstacle to overcome, I now realize that having such a talented older sibling has been a gift. Just his presence has given me the motivation to achieve. The competitive spirit that helps me excel in all I do originated with him. Today, I no longer compare myself to see who is smarter or "better." I realize that I have made a name for myself through my own achievements and successes, and now know that being "Jordan's little sister" isn't such a bad thing after all.

54. "Billy" by Paige Kouba

Getting to know Billy was an ordeal for me. I had never encountered someone so belligerent, underhanded and mean. His eyes would narrow in disgust every time we met, and frequently I caught him sticking out his tongue behind my back. Billy was the most antagonistic duck I had ever met.

Our tortured relationship began last summer, when I was working for my neighbor Charlie in his sustenance garden. Charlie was a true master of the art, and when he asked if I would help him a few times a week, I instantly agreed. I gained a lot from a summer's worth of manual labor; though I didn't make any money, my wages were paid in vegetables, beautiful sunrises, and knowledge.

There was so much to learn. Charlie was not one to spray his beds with MiracleGro and cross his fingers. His enlightened permaculture relied on an understanding of plants from their topmost seedpods to their tiniest roots. His breadth of knowledge encompassed more than just vegetables—our morning chores started with feeding the animals of this tiny Eden. Each day, we let out chickens, gathered eggs, hayed bunnies, and fed fish, with Billy the guard duck marching behind.

Poor Billy was the ugly duckling who never grew into a swan.

He stood about three feet high, and every inch was just unsightly. His bitter heart matched his warty, mottled exterior, and he would periodically waddle up behind me to bite me in the calf if I wasn't paying attention. Fiercely territorial, he fancied himself the sentinel of the garden, but he was largely docile as long as Charlie, the alpha-male, was around.

When Charlie went away for a week, I agreed to look after his property. I felt ready to step in for him as overseer of the garden, but Billy saw an opportunity to move up the social ladder. Upon arriving on the first day, I heard the sinister hiss of the vengeful demon-duck. Billy's feathery head crest stood erect, a sure sign that he had entered battle mode.

The ensuing dance of attack and retreat led us around the garden several times. I tried in vain to perform my chores, but he was unrelenting, and getting bolder. In desperation, I whirled around, resolved to face my challenger. I grabbed a handy trashcan for a shield.

"If you don't behave," I threatened, "I will put you under this bucket and sit on it."

I inched forward, talking him down like a hostage negotiator. My heart skipped a beat as he cocked his head, as if sizing up his chances for a deathblow. This was it. I was doomed.

Then his crest feathers relaxed. He turned, waggled his tail, and shuffled away, feigning indifference. I had won.

By the time Charlie returned a week later, Billy the bully had been subdued. I told Charlie with pride that all had run smoothly during my week as alpha-duck; I had earned my place in the pecking order.

55. "Refrigerator" by Paige Kouba

DO NOT EAT ANYTHING FROM THE BOTTOM SHELF OF THE MINI-FRIDGE. I'm testing the effects of various pollutants on populations of rotifers and I would hate for you to become my next trial. It's for that environmental studies class I was telling you about, the one with the amazing professor; she let me take home some of the extra samples after she did the lab demo, as long as I promised I was about to make a scientific breakthrough. We just finished a unit on water storage and treatment in less-developed countries, and for our midterm, we had to start from scratch and design a low-cost system that a given village could use to purify its drinking water. It's my favorite class by far, but I'll bet you've guessed that after hearing about it nonstop all quarter.

If you're reading this, I am probably still out on a run. The coach has been really good about balancing our training schedule with exam week, so we aren't actually meeting for practice, but I just have to get out for a while. Morning runs are the best thing for stress relief, and I still can't get over how beautiful this city is right after sunrise. I won't be longer than an hour or so, but if I miss you, good luck on the rest of your exams today! If you still want to go over the Spanish notes tonight, I am definitely up for it, even if we just end up discussing our dinner plans en español again.

¡Hasta luego, dude!

--Paige

P.S. Sara from the end of the hall wanted to know if she could borrow the unicycle, but I still haven't figured out how to patch the leaky inner tube. Can you help me with it this weekend if you're not busy?

56. "Untitled" by Jake Stepansky

I cried when I heard Regina Spektor's song "Firewood" for the first time. I cried when Will Smith and his son had to spend the night in a train station restroom in "The Pursuit of Happyness." I cried when I closed the book "Extremely Loud and Incredibly Close," and I cried when they closed my grandfather's coffin.

What truly moves me feels essential to who I am. And I have come to believe that all the varied ways – joyful, elated, sad, complicated – in which each of us are moved are also personal, telling, and uniquely us. There may be no better way to get to know someone than by asking, "What moves you?"

For me, on one level, that question could easily provoke the response of "my legs." As a rower, I rely greatly on these appendages – paradoxically more than my arms – to accelerate down the Schuylkill River during a race. When I am in my boat, working in perfect unison with three of my closest friends to propel our vessel across the course, I feel like I am flying – both physically and emotionally. For I have found that along with the passionate application of time, power, and energy toward a goal comes a deeply spiritual and organic release. And so I am not only moved physically by my oar, but also am inspired by the grace of the human body and the beauty of the simultaneous tension and catharsis that accompanies a focused physical exertion.

Beyond the realm of athleticism, I am passionately moved by music and literature. My favorite books have inspired tears, and their imagery has left indelible impressions. Upon reading Elie Wiesel's *Night* in eighth grade, the scene of Elie's father's death so close to their liberation from Auschwitz illuminated for me the brevity and preciousness of life, and, consequently, the importance of loving without falter or fail. When my own life was touched by the sudden passing of a beloved school theater director, these themes deeply resonated, along with the urgency of keeping and cultivating community to transcend loss.

I am moved by the immense capacity of the arts to serve as a catalyst for cross-cultural connection. I observe this every day at my high school, where, despite its ethnic diversity, many extracurricular groups have unconsciously sorted themselves by race. Our vibrant arts community is an exception – a multicolored, multicultural hub of acceptance – which, for some of my friends with troubled home lives and overwhelming economic strain, is all that tethers them to the goal of completing their high school education. The loving bonds formed in this community of students who are committed not only to their art but to each other – including those who join me yearly, dropping in to create our musical revue together rather than dropping out – has given me insight not only into the centrality of friendship and cooperation, but also into the profound power of art to shape and transform lives.

All these things, in enduring ways, move me – to action, to tears, and to the finish line. But it is, in truth, the act of sharing these things with others – seeing their faces light up with recognition and connection, and finding out what moves *them* so much that they simply have to share it with me too – which moves me most of all.

57. "Ink" by Daniel Windham

Last night I was thinking about ink. When rain falls on a handwritten page, the ink spreads out a bit, loses its crispness. It's rarely pleasant. But every now and then, hidden colors emerge. Suddenly you discover that simple black ink is green and shades of blue and a fragile pink edge. If some being creates us or writes the stories of our lives, this ink crafts it all, and in just the right rainfall all the colors resurface.

That was my passing thought as I lay waiting for sleep.

So I wrote it down. Too many good ideas occur and get forgotten and disappear without a chance to bloom; I choose to capture mine, and pursue them.

The notebook next to my bed has no theme beyond that – the ideas set down in it range from business strategies to quickly sketched designs for artwork, tech products to personal goals, quotations to... just about anything. Schematics for a "digital highlighter" succeed a note regarding stocks, while other sheets host sculptural designs inspired by lines in the palm of my hand. Satires of various family members flood nine pages. One idea asserts the optimum way for a restaurant to serve ice cream sundaes.

Now it may be I never build the fountain I've imagined – one with spoons oriented to catch streams of water and fan them out like umbrellas. (I'd certainly like to, but who can say for sure?) But here's the thing: I don't wait around when creative thoughts seize me. I leap at them impulsively, intuitively, and as I bore into them my senses hum vibrant-alive. The moment after an idea for an essay or book pierces me is the moment I open Microsoft Word; I scramble for pen and paper the instant I see a ripple or twist of light for artistic depiction.

And once entangled in a complex problem I attack it, Hercules wrestling serpents, marbled Laocoön in defiance. I rage against the physics or calculus problem that stumps my classmates (they who go gentle into the night), and more often than not I emerge victorious. I assail the New York Times' 7x7 KenKen every Sunday. In AP Language last year, I elected to write my final project (a persuasive speech) satirically. Though I had never written a satirical argument before, I undertook to entertain my audience while presenting a rock-solid argument in favor of tenure. I drafted, cut, and reworked text for twenty-eight hours to forge my fifteen-minute speech. I ultimately asserted that tenure countered the American tradition of grossly underpaying teachers; that the tenure-sheltered free will of teachers was preventing states from homogenizing and force-feeding patriotism to citizens (actions that Huxley and Orwell demonstrated are the keys to any ideal civilization); that only under the academic freedom of tenure may teachers spread "lies" such as evolution and the Holocaust. The class loved my speech. I loved working for it, feeling the thrill of a true challenge.

If I am composed of ink, the black conglomerate shows that I've been an outgoing leader and academically successful. A hundred hundred inks look no different. Yet diffract me: the shades of blue are my ever-branching interests, the rippling surging rivers of my curiosity, kneaded by the rushing winds of the world. The emerald green glow is my pulsing energy, like bright coals and strong bellows, at once flames and inflammatory: my vigorous passion to create and my ceaseless drive to achieve. And my pink edge – that's the secret key, the most hidden yet most integral, the uniting, driving force behind it all. It's my enjoyment. I love finding possibilities that no one else sees, improving something as no one else did, solving problems that no one else knew existed. I won't tell you when I've done so, nor explain why I was up until two in the morning when to you nothing seems changed – but I'll know. I would have gotten an A on that paper anyway, sure; but I knew it wasn't right, and moreover, I knew how to make it right. To me, pursuing the solution to a complex problem is the most fulfilling thing. That's when I'm happiest. And that is my edge.

Perhaps I seem at first a nondescript black – but wait until my hues shine through.

58. "Tennis" by Daniel Windham

At the corner of each eye lie little crinkle lines, tip-offs to her mood: they might be laughing, or exhausted, or some days furious and fed up with people. If she's worried about her own affairs she tries to hide it, but rarely can. She never hides her anger, her glee, or her fierce, well-deserved pride. She never hides her opinions.

Kim Grant began in South Africa, on a farm. It was a four-hour drive to tennis, and she never missed a practice. She fought all the way to Wimbledon, to number 76 in the world. Then she moved to the United States and built a tennis academy from scratch.

Before I began training with Kim, my motivation depended strictly on my interest. If I found my class interesting, I worked at it. When an idea intrigued me, I pursued it. But I avoided working for some theoretical "later."

Kim made me want to change that. I wanted her discipline and motivation. I yearned to know the agony of fighting for something month after month, the drive necessary to dive into something and claw all the way through without ever pausing for breath. I dove into tennis. If Saturday morning Kim wanted me at 7:45, I was there. If Wednesday night she wanted me past 8:00, I texted my parents to have dinner without me. Every day I played tennis I fought to develop Kim's drive, and after four years I caught hold of it.

Paradoxically, this led me to quit tennis. I had always played because I enjoyed exercise and the thrill of competition. I loved the people involved and the work to improve myself. Yet finding the discipline to truly achieve forced me to reconsider my goals: what did I plan to achieve? Kim became a professional athlete, but that wasn't my aspiration.

So for now, I'm working on my school's food drive. I'm focusing on my classes; I'm tutoring; I'm drawing a lot. I'm searching for my next pursuit. When I find it, I'll fight for it – and no matter how long it takes, I'll get it. The course of my life may not be altered by what I learned of tennis, but the dedication, respect for work, and purpose in action I learned under Kim will resonate always.

Occasionally she still calls to ask if I can help her out, moving furniture into the office or driving kids to other courts. People tell me I'm crazy for doing it, and crazier still not to let her pay me. But I think back to every morning Kim let me hit when there wasn't a clinic, or freed a court so I could practice serving. I think of everything Kim taught me.

I do not grant loyalty freely, but when I grant it, I give it completely. Kim has been my tennis coach, and I am thankful for it; but Kim has also been my mentor, my role model – and I am forever grateful for it.

About the Compilers

Jordan Tung

By strategically crafting every aspect of his applications to distinguish himself from other applicants, Jordan was admitted to every school on his "Reach" list, including Harvard, Yale, Princeton, Stanford, Brown, Columbia, Cornell and UPenn. Four years later, Jordan graduated from Harvard University and quickly realized his passion for helping others succeed. Drawing from his experience as the child of a single mother in a humble household, Jordan founded EmpiricEdge, hoping to provide average families with competitively priced, individualized and results-driven services. Having given talks about college admissions and essays writing at dozens of public and private institutions, Jordan hopes that this compilation of successful essays will show students how to separate themselves from the pack.

Kevin Jain

After graduating as valedictorian of his high school class and receiving admission to nearly every school he applied to, Kevin matriculated at Harvard and quickly fell in love with the distinguished classes, classmates, and experiences afforded to him. While in school, Kevin founded the Harvard College Future Society, the first campus organization of its kind, to consider the long-term implications of technology and its impact on society. He holds professional experience working for several major Finance, Venture Capital, and Entrepreneurship firms around the country. Kevin attributes his success in the college application process to a combination of diligence, creativity, and being able to share his genuine voice in his admissions essays. Kevin is sharing this book with the hopes that it helps prospective students see how they can share their own voice in their application and find a quality education at the school of their dreams.

480-540-5657

<u>Katy</u>

@ Katy James sikims@gmail.com @

3 other people

@ 99 $ 1/month 1 Ran

|———————|

Made in the USA
Middletown, DE
18 October 2017